FLAVOURS

the essence of entertaining

THE COOKBOOK

FLAVOURS – The Cookbook

published by:
Centax Books/Publishing Solutions, a division of PrintWest Communications Ltd.

First Printing – November 2006

Copyright © 2006 by:
PrintWest Communications Ltd.

Library and Archives Canada Cataloguing in Publication

Flavours : the cookbook : the essence of entertaining / magazine editor, Brandon Boone ; cookbook editor, Margo Embury.

Recipes from the Canadian magazine Flavours.

ISBN 13: 978-1-897010-36-5
ISBN 10: 1-897010-36-2

1. Cookery. I. Boone, Brandon II. Embury, Margo

TX714.F626 2006   641.5   C2006-905653-6

Cover/Page Design, Formatting and Index by:
Iona Glabus,
Centax Books

Cover Photograph by:
Brian Gould,
Brian Gould Photography Inc.

Designed, Printed and Produced in Canada by:
Centax Books, a division of PrintWest Communications Ltd.
Publishing Director: Margo Embury
1150 Eighth Avenue, Regina, Saskatchewan, Canada S4R 1C9
(306) 359-7580   FAX (306) 359-6443
E-mail: centax@printwest.com   www.centaxbooks.com

TABLE OF CONTENTS

Recipes have been tested in U.S. Standard measurements. Common metric measurements are given as a convenience for those who are more familiar with metric. Recipes have not been tested in metric.

INTRODUCTION

Brandon Boone

It's funny how dreams can sometimes turn into reality.

Three years ago, a good friend of mine, a fellow whom I regularly tortured in college by eating my gourmet lunches in front of, called me up out of the blue with an opportunity that, frankly, still shocks me today.

Before even getting to the important question, he began by asking if I was still in the habit of bringing said lunches to work.

Of course, that was like asking if water was wet.

He was actually calling to see if I'd be interested in running a food and drink publication that would showcase culinary talent across the Prairies.

The only sound heard in response was the phone hitting the floor.

After regaining my composure (and my motor skills) I picked up the phone and made him repeat the question. Even though he said exactly the same thing, I thought for sure there was still something I was missing.

This kind of phone call is akin to having the person on the other end of the line telling you that you've won the lottery.

I finally managed to stammer, "yes."

In a nutshell, that's how *Flavours* magazine was born.

From there, a raft of talented designers, managers and salespeople started work on the project, to actually bring it to life. Aside from those working within our company walls, we were fortunate enough to find and recruit some fantastic food writers, incredible chefs and talented photographers from across the Prairies to contribute to the magazine. All of our efforts were rewarded when the very first issue hit store shelves and, subsequently, flew off them.

We've since grown and expanded to include British Columbia, which joins us in celebrating its local bounty and talent.

One of the things that makes *Flavours* unique is that even through we're distributed throughout Western Canada, we can still bring you stories and recipes from people living in your community. A lot of people aren't aware that the issue of *Flavours* available in British Columbia is different from those available in Manitoba, Saskatchewan and Alberta. That's because we have writers and photographers on the ground in each of those provinces, ensuring your regional culinary voice is heard.

For the past three years, it has been my privilege to hear your stories and test the recipes submitted to the magazine, many of which have gone on to become my personal favourites. The diversity of ingredients and recipes I've seen is a testament to how creative Canadians can be when it comes to cooking.

I've always loved food and the way it binds people together. To this day, I can still smell the aroma of my mother's Sunday roasts, a meal I continue to have at home today. My dad also contributed to my fascination with food. After our swimming lessons, he used to make great snack plates of assorted cheeses, cured meats and various raw vegetables. But it's not the flavours that I remember the most fondly, it's the time spent with my family in the kitchen–helping, laughing and loving.

Today, that respect and admiration for the way food brings people together remains and is very much entrenched in the way I live. The joy, yes joy, that a meal made from scratch brings to those who share in it is undeniable. The people at your table don't have to be foodies or even people who cook all the time–anyone who takes a fork to his or her mouth with a morsel of something you've just finished making knows it's special. Would they have the same reaction to a store-bought meal you've just pulled out of the microwave? Highly unlikely.

We are very fortunate to be able to access fresh food practically whenever we want. That being said, I think very few people are actually doing so and, instead, take this privilege for granted. There's no question that making food from scratch takes more effort than dialing a phone or nuking a frozen dinner from the supermarket. But what I don't understand is how people can compare the flavours of a meal made by your hands against one in the fancy packaging–they're not even close.

The other argument is time, which I think is no argument at all. Sure, there are recipes that require a full day of marinating or some with enough chopping to tax even the most industrious cooks. But, there are also thousands that can be made in less than 30 minutes. If you think about it, that's less time than it takes for a pizza to arrive at your door.

Inside *Flavours : The Cookbook* you're going to find all kinds of recipes–some will inspire the novice cook and others will intrigue the seasoned chef, but all of them are truly worthwhile and delicious. We've spent a great deal of time researching these recipes, testing and tweaking them to ensure they are the very best. Many have been created by western Canada's finest chefs; others originate from kitchens and homes throughout Western Canada, from people you might know, neighbours, even friends. We've put them all together in one place so that you can see and experience the culinary innovation coming out of these four provinces.

It's been really tough, if you call eating and drinking your way through hundreds of outstanding recipes difficult, putting together this cookbook for you. There have been so many fantastic meals to consider that it was difficult to choose which ones to include. In the end, we've picked the best of *Flavours* magazine for you to enjoy again, or for the first time.

I'd like to thank a few people who helped bring this cookbook together:

First, my wife, Rachel Boone, my unofficial taste-taster as well as counsel, advocate and love of my life;

Dan Marce, who, as publisher, has provided unstinting guidance and support for *Flavours* magazine;

Margo Embury, whose patience, expertise and diligence was a driving force behind this cookbook;

Iona Glabus, whose technical expertise and design skills have created every page of *Flavours : The Cookbook*;

Joan McCannel, PrintWest's indefatigable customer service rep., who has shepherded every issue of *Flavours* magazine, plus this cookbook, through the myriad details of the printing process;

Grant Crosbie, über-sales manager and friend;

Judy Fowler, our exceptionally talented and creative food stylist whose magic makes the recipes jump off the page;

Brian Gould, our lead and cover photographer whose enthusiasm, commitment and expertise has helped shape the magazine you see today;

Hamid Attie, Patricia Holdsworth and John Ulan: our hardworking and diligent regional photographers who also capture the people, places and food featured in *Flavours*.

And, especially, thank you to the hundreds of contributors who have shared their passion for food and drink with us so we can share it with you.

In closing, I'll leave you with one of my favourite quotes by Alan Richmond:

"Food is life. The rest is parsley."

Brandon Boone
Editor-in-Chief
Flavours magazine

BREAKFAST
.... Brunch & Lunch

Whole-Wheat & Toasted Pecan Waffles with Glazed Bananas

This is a fabulous recipe that will become an immediate family favourite, but it does require the use of a waffle maker.

3/4 cup (175 mL) finely chopped pecans
1 1/4 cups (300 mL) whole-wheat flour
3/4 cup (175 mL) all-purpose white flour
1 tbsp (15 mL) light brown sugar
1 tbsp (15 mL) honey
1 tbsp (15 mL) baking powder
1/2 tsp (2 mL) kosher salt
1/2 tsp (2 mL) baking soda
2 cups (500 mL) 2 percent milk
1/3 cup plus 1 tbsp (90 mL) vegetable oil
2 eggs

Glazed Bananas:
2 tbsp (30 mL) unsalted butter
2 large, firm, ripe bananas cut into 1/4" (6 mm) slices
1 tbsp (15 mL) brown sugar
1 cup (250 mL) pure maple syrup

● ● ● ●

Preheat waffle maker to desired setting. In a skillet over medium-low heat, toast pecan pieces until lightly browned and fragrant. Remove from heat. In a large mixing bowl, combine all ingredients. With an electric mixer, mix on low speed for 4 minutes, scraping sides often. Let rest 5 minutes. Pour batter into waffle maker and cook as per manufacturer's recommendation.

Bananas: Melt butter in a large non-stick skillet over medium-high heat. Toss banana slices with brown sugar; add banana slices to skillet in 1 layer and cook until golden, approximately 1 minute per side. Remove skillet from heat and add syrup. Spoon bananas over waffles; drizzle with warm syrup before serving.

● ● ● ●

MAKES 8 WAFFLES

Recipe by Brandon Boone
Photography: Brian Gould

Apricot & Almond Stuffed French Toast with Orange Drizzle

Orange Drizzle:
1/3 cup (75 mL) frozen orange juice concentrate
1/4 cup (60 mL) butter
1/4 cup (60 mL) white sugar

4, 1" (2.5 cm) thick slices of French bread
2 tbsp (30 mL) diced dried apricot
2 tbsp (30 mL) chopped, toasted almonds
1/2 cup (125 mL) ricotta cheese
2 tbsp (30 mL) mozzarella cheese
1 tbsp (15 mL) light brown sugar
1/2 tsp (2 mL) vanilla extract
2 eggs
1/2 cup (125 mL) milk
1 tbsp (15 mL) butter

• • • •

Drizzle: Combine orange juice concentrate, butter and sugar in a small saucepan. Stir over low heat until butter melts and sugar dissolves (do not boil). Remove from heat and keep warm.

Cut a horizontal slit through each bread slice to form a pocket; be careful not to cut through the other side. In a bowl, combine apricots, almonds, cheeses, sugar and vanilla. Stuff 2 tbsp (30 mL) of apricot mixture into each bread slice, spreading over pocket. In a large shallow dish, beat eggs; add milk and mix to combine. Place stuffed bread in dish, turning to coat. Repeat with remaining slices.

In a non-stick skillet over medium heat, melt butter. Gently place the stuffed bread in the skillet, cooking 3 minutes or until browned. Flip bread and repeat. Add additional butter to the skillet as necessary and cook remaining slices.

Serve French Toast topped with Orange Drizzle.

• • • •

SERVES 4

Recipe by Brandon Boone
Photography: Brian Gould

(S)panish Potato Tortilla with Lemon Hollandaise

Tortilla is a fairly bland tapas bar offering. Roasted red pepper and parsley provide perk without straying too far from the traditional. However, the accompanying lemon hollandaise does stray rather far from the classic (but oh so deliciously). Try this for a holiday brunch with ham or peameal bacon.

Tortilla:
1/2 cup (125 mL) olive oil
1 cup (250 mL) sliced onion
2 lbs (1 kg) Yukon Gold potatoes, peeled and sliced into 1/4" (5 mm) thick slices
6 eggs
1 1/2 tsp (7 mL) salt
1/4 tsp (1 mL) freshly ground black pepper
1 large sweet red pepper, roasted, peeled, seeded and cut into strips
2 tbsp (30 mL) chopped fresh parsley

Lemon Hollandaise:
1 cup (250 mL) salted butter
3 egg yolks
1 tbsp (15 mL) milk
1 tbsp (15 mL) fresh lemon juice
pinch of cayenne

● ○ ● ○

Tortilla: Heat oil in heatproof skillet over medium heat. When hot, carefully add onions and potatoes. Reduce heat to medium-low to low and cook gently, turning occasionally for 20 to 25 minutes, or until potatoes are translucent and onions softened. Using a slotted spoon remove potatoes and onions to a large mixing bowl. Drain pan but reserve oil. Scrape any potato off pan; wipe pan with a paper towel. Preheat oven to 350°F (180°C). Beat eggs with salt and pepper; pour over potato mixture. Add red pepper strips and parsley; using a folding motion, mix well. Return pan to stove; add some of the drained oil to generously coat bottom. When hot, add potato mixture, smoothing top. Cook 10 minutes over medium-low heat, or just until edges are set. Bake in oven for 15 minutes.

Hollandaise: In a small mixing bowl, melt butter in a microwave for approximately 1 minute. Place egg yolks and milk in blender; whirl briefly. While whirling at high speed, add half of hot butter in a steady stream; mixture will become milky. Whirl in lemon juice and cayenne, then whirl in remaining butter, adding in a steady stream.

Loosen tortilla and turn onto a warmed plate; cut into 8 wedges. Serve wedges on warmed plates with a spoonful of hollandaise.

● ○ ● ○

SERVES 8

Recipe by Marilyn Bentz Crowley
Photography: Brian Gould

(P)olenta with Chorizo, Feta & Spanish Eggs

Italian, Spanish and Greek ingredients combine for a flavourful breakfast dish.

3 1/4 cups (765 mL) water
1 cup (250 mL) coarse polenta
2 cups (500 mL) corn kernels
salt and pepper, to taste
6 oz (170 g) creamy Greek-style feta
1/3 cup (75 mL) chopped fresh cilantro
1 lb (500 g) chorizo sausage, casings removed
28 oz (798 mL) can diced tomatoes
14 oz (398 mL) can black beans, drained, rinsed
juice of 1 lime

Spanish Eggs:
1 tbsp (15 mL) butter
1 yellow banana pepper, sliced into rounds,
   1/8" (3 mm) thick
2 green onions, roughly chopped
6 eggs
2 ripe Roma tomatoes, seeded and diced
1 tsp (5 mL) EACH, ground cumin and oregano
1 tbsp (15 mL) chopped fresh cilantro
salt and pepper, to taste

● ○ ○ ○

Preheat oven to 425°F (220°C). Combine water, polenta and corn kernels in a 9 x 13" (23 x 33 cm) baking dish; season with salt and pepper and mix well. Bake until all the water is absorbed and polenta is tender, stirring once, approximately 30 minutes.

Toss feta and cilantro in small bowl.

Cook sausage in a skillet over medium-high heat until browned, breaking it into small pieces. Add tomatoes to skillet and reduce heat to medium; simmer for 15 to 20 minutes, or until liquid has reduced. Add black beans and simmer for 5 minutes longer, or until heated through. Drizzle sausage mixture with lime juice.

Eggs: Melt butter in a non-stick skillet over medium-high heat. Add banana pepper and green onion to skillet and sauté for 2 minutes. Remove from skillet and, using a paper towel, wipe skillet surface. Return to heat and add eggs. In the skillet, break egg yolks and stir gently; let eggs begin to set before stirring again. Continue to cook until egg is fully cooked; add banana pepper mixture, tomatoes, cumin, oregano and cilantro. Toss together until heated through.

In the centre of each of 4 plates, place a 3" (8 cm) square of polenta. Top with chorizo mixture, cheese mixture and Spanish eggs. Serve immediately.

● ○ ● ○

SERVES 4

Recipe by Brandon Boone
Photography: Brian Gould

Ham & Sharp Cheddar Biscuits

These quick biscuits make divine toppers for chicken potpie and are also great on their own – hot from the oven.

1/2 cup (125 mL) minced onion
1 tbsp (15 mL) butter
2 cups (500 mL) all-purpose flour
1 tbsp (15 mL) baking powder
1 tsp (5 mL) kosher salt
1/2 tsp (2 mL) baking soda
1/4 cup (60 mL) unsalted butter, cut
    into 1/4" (6 mm) cubes
1 1/2 cups (375 mL) buttermilk
1/2 cup (125 mL) diced cooked ham
1/2 cup (125 mL) grated sharp
    Cheddar
additional flour for your hands
2 tbsp (30 mL) unsalted butter,
    melted

● ● ● ●

Preheat oven to 500°F (260°C). Line a baking sheet with parchment paper.

Combine onion and butter in a skillet over medium-low heat and cook until tender but not browned, about 5 minutes; let cool. In a bowl, combine flour, baking powder, salt and baking soda; add butter and mix with your fingers until mealy in texture. Add the onions, buttermilk, ham and cheese, stirring in with a spatula until just incorporated (it should be a bit loose).

Scoop out batter with a large spoon to form 12 biscuits and lightly shape them with floured hands. Arrange biscuits close together on the baking sheet for soft biscuits, or spread them apart for crisper biscuits. Brush with hot melted butter. Bake 5 minutes then reduce temperature to 450°F (230°C) and bake 15 minutes, or until deep golden brown. Cool in pan for several minutes then invert onto a kitchen towel. Turn right side up and break apart. Serve hot.

● ● ● ●

MAKES 12 BISCUITS

Recipe by dee Hobsbawn-Smith
Photography: Brian Gould

Cheddar Cornbread with Kernels & Chives

People in the United States Deep South are experts on hot, humid summer days when appetites need to be jump-started with strong flavours – these cornbread squares do just that!

1 small ear fresh corn, roasted
1 cup (250 mL) cornmeal
1 1/2 cups (375 mL) milk
1 cup (250 mL) all-purpose flour
2 tbsp (30 mL) granulated sugar
2 tsp (10 mL) baking powder
1/2 tsp (2 mL) salt
2 eggs
1 tbsp (15 mL) EACH, melted butter and canola oil
1/2 cup (125 mL) snipped chives OR thinly sliced green onion
1 cup (250 mL) grated Cheddar cheese

● ○ ● ○

Using a sharp knife, cut kernels from corncob by standing cob on the broad end and cutting down. Measure out 1 cup (250 mL) kernels.

Preheat oven to 425°F (220°C). Liberally coat a 9" (23 cm) square or 8 x 12" (20 x 30 cm) baking dish with non-stick cooking spray.

In a large mixing bowl, soak cornmeal in milk while assembling remaining ingredients. Combine flour with sugar, baking powder and salt. Separate eggs; whites into a small mixing bowl and yolks stirred into the wet cornmeal mixture. Beat egg whites until soft peaks form when beaters are lifted. Add flour mixture to cornmeal mixture. Stir in butter and oil until blended; stir in kernels and onion. Fold whites into batter until just combined. Pour batter into prepared baking dish; smooth top and sprinkle with cheese. Bake 23 to 25 minutes, or until golden with edges pulling away from the sides. Place on a rack to cool slightly, then cut. Serve warm, topped with a sprinkle of additional snipped chives.

● ○ ● ○

MAKES 24 TO 36 SQUARES

Recipe by Marilyn Bentz Crowley

Photography: Brian Gould

Pair With:
• Brown Ale
• German Sylvaner
• B.C. Riesling

ienna-Style Focaccia

10 oz (300 mL) Vienna-style beer
3 oz (90 mL) Italian dressing
20 oz (600 mL) lukewarm water
1/2 tsp (2 mL) oregano
1/2 tsp (2 mL) thyme
1/2 tsp (2 mL) basil
2 tbsp (30 mL) yeast
1 1/2 tbsp (22 mL) sugar
2 tsp (10 mL) salt
1 3/4 lb (875 g) flour

● ● ● ●

Warm beer for 1 minute in the microwave. Warm Italian dressing in a microwave for 20 seconds. Combine all ingredients except flour in a mixing bowl; stir well to combine. Add flour and stir well to combine. Using an electric mixer, mix contents on low for about 5 to 10 minutes, adding more flour until the mixture is just sticking to the side of the bowl. Cover with a damp towel and let rise for 1 hour. Divide dough into 3 equal portions; shape into flat rounds. Let rise for 30 to 45 more minutes. Push down gently. Preheat oven to 375°F (190°C).

Let rise again for about 30 to 40 minutes more. Poke 5 holes in the top of each loaf. Liberally brush each top with olive before placing in oven. Bake for 19 minutes.

● ● ● ●

MAKES 3 LOAVES

Recipe by The Regina Bushwakker Brewpub
Photography: Brian Gould

Pair With:
• Italina Moretti
• German Pilsner
• Alberta Wheat Beer

hole-Wheat Pizza Dough

2 1/4 cups (560 mL) whole-wheat flour, divided
1/2 tsp (2 mL) EACH, sugar and salt
2 tsp (10 mL) instant or quick-rise yeast
1 tbsp (15 mL) canola oil
3/4 cup (175 mL) water
cornmeal for sprinkling

● ○ ● ○

Combine 2 cups (500 mL) flour, sugar, salt and yeast in a large bowl. Combine oil and water in a measuring cup. Make a well in centre of dry ingredients and pour water mixture into centre of the well. Gradually mix ingredients to form a soft dough. Add remaining flour as needed. Turn dough out onto a floured board and knead until soft and elastic, about 8 to 10 minutes. Dough should be slightly sticky but should-n't stick to your hands. Let dough rest, covered, on the counter for 10 to 15 minutes. Roll out dough to fit pizza pan. Sprinkle pan with cornmeal. Carefully place dough on pan. Add toppings of your choice and bake according to recipes following.

● ○ ● ○

Recipe by Judy Fowler

asic Tomato Sauce

2 tbsp (30 mL) olive oil
2 large onions, peeled and finely chopped
2 garlic cloves, peeled and finely chopped
2 lbs (1 kg) ripe tomatoes
2 tbsp (30 mL) chopped fresh basil
salt and pepper to taste
dash of sugar

● ○ ● ○

Heat oil in a non-stick skillet over medium-low heat; cook onions and garlic for about 10 minutes, or until onions are translucent. Finely chop tomatoes and add to onion mixture. Add basil, salt, pepper and sugar. Cook over medium heat for 35 to 40 minutes, or until sauce thickens. Remove from heat and let cool to room temperature before using.

● ○ ● ○

MAKES 4 CUPS

Recipe by Judy Fowler
Photography: Brian Gould

rtichoke, Bocconcini & Pesto Pizza

1 recipe Whole-Wheat Pizza Dough, page 15
1 cup (250 mL) Basic Tomato Sauce, page 15
3 tbsp (45 mL) basil pesto
2 balls fresh bocconcini cheese, sliced
2 plum tomatoes, thinly sliced
3 tbsp (45 mL) chopped fresh oregano
1 small jar marinated artichoke hearts, drained, quartered
1/4 cup (60 mL) freshly grated Parmesan cheese

● ● ● ●

Roll out pizza crust and place on cornmeal-dusted pizza pan. Spread tomato sauce over top. Using a teaspoon, drop small amounts of pesto randomly over tomato sauce. Top with bocconcini, tomatoes, oregano and artichokes. Sprinkle with Parmesan cheese. Bake pizza at 450°F (230°C) for about 15 minutes, or until pizza is golden on the edges and crisp underneath.

● ● ● ●

Recipe by Judy Fowler
Photography: Brian Gould

Pair With:
• Italian Greco di Tufo
• Grüner Veltliner
• B.C. Pinot Gris

Coconut, Peanut & Prawn Pizza

3/4 cup (175 mL) peanut butter
1 cup (250 mL) unsweetened coconut milk
2 tbsp (30 mL) cornstarch
2 tbsp (30 mL) EACH, water and fish sauce
1 recipe Whole-Wheat Pizza Dough, page 15
8 oz (250 g) jumbo shrimp, cooked, peeled and coarsely chopped
6 green onions, chopped, divided
1/3 cup (75 mL) fresh basil leaves
1 red pepper, finely julienned
2 tbsp (30 mL) chopped cilantro
2 cups (500 mL) bean sprouts, divided
2 cups (500 mL) shredded mozzarella cheese
1 lime, cut into wedges
1/4 cup (60 mL) chopped peanuts, toasted

● ● ● ●

In a medium saucepan, whisk together peanut butter and coconut milk. Place over medium heat and cook stirring constantly. Whisk together cornstarch and water. Add to peanut butter mixture. Add fish sauce. Bring to a boil to thicken. Remove from heat and let cool.

Roll out pizza crust and place on cornmeal-dusted pizza pan. Spread sauce over crust. Sprinkle shrimp, half of green onions, basil, red pepper, cilantro and half of bean sprouts over sauce. Sprinkle cheese over toppings. Sprinkle remaining green onions, bean sprouts and peanuts on top of cheese. Bake pizza at 400°F (200°C) for about 15 minutes, or until pizza is golden on the edges and crisp underneath.

● ● ● ●

Recipe by Judy Fowler

Photography: Brian Gould

Pair With:
• Italian Pinot Grigio
• Alsace Pinot Gris
• B.C. Gewürztraminer

(P)ancetta, Kalamata Olive & Monterey Jack Pizza

1 recipe Whole-Wheat Pizza Dough, page 15
1 cup (250 mL) Basic Tomato Sauce, page 15
6 oz (175 g) smoked ham, thinly sliced
4 oz (120 g) pancetta, thinly sliced
1 cup (250 mL) grated Monterey Jack cheese
1/2 cup (125 mL) crumbled blue cheese
1 cup (250 mL) cherry tomatoes, cut in half
1/3 cup (75 mL) pine nuts
1 tbsp (15 mL) fresh rosemary needles
3/4 cup (175 mL) kalamata olives, pits removed, halved

● ● ● ●

Roll out pizza crust and place on cornmeal-dusted pizza pan. Spread tomato sauce over crust. Arrange remaining ingredients over pizza in order listed. Bake at 450°F (230°C) for about 15 minutes, or until pizza is golden on the edges and crisp underneath.

● ● ● ●

Recipe by Judy Fowler

Photography: Brian Gould

Pair With:
• Italian Chianti Classico
• California Sangiovese
• Nut Brown Ale

Savoyard Ham, Crème Fraiche & Potato Pizza

Crème fraiche and potatoes on a pizza? This is truly wonderful.

Dough:
2 tbsp (30 mL) yeast
2 tbsp (30 mL) sugar
1 1/2 cups (375 mL) warm-to-hot
  water, divided
4 cups (1 L) all-purpose flour
1 tbsp (15 mL) kosher salt
1 tsp (5 mL) dried thyme OR
  herbes de Provence
2 tbsp (30 mL) olive oil

cornmeal for sprinkling
1 cup (250 mL) sautéed sliced onion
1 cup (250 mL) diced cooked ham
1 cup (250 mL) sliced or chopped crisply
  cooked bacon
1 cup (250 mL) pitted, chopped Niçoise OR kalamata olives
2 cups (500 mL) sliced, cooked Yukon Gold potatoes
2 tsp (10 mL) dried herbes de Provence
1 cup (250 mL) crème fraiche OR whipping cream
2 cups (500 mL) grated Gruyère, Jarlsberg or Fontina cheese
extra-virgin olive oil
kosher salt and freshly cracked black pepper

● ● ● ●

Dough: In a countertop mixer bowl, combine yeast, sugar and 1/2 cup (125 mL) water. Let stand for about 5 minutes, until it is puffy. Add flour, salt, herbs and remaining water. Mix well. Turn dough onto counter and knead well for 5 to 10 minutes, or until dough is smooth and elastic.

Pour oil into mixing bowl, swirl it around to coat sides and bottom and place dough in bowl. Roll dough in oil so entire surface is lightly covered. Cover bowl with plastic wrap and let dough rise until doubled in bulk, 30 to 60 minutes, depending on room temperature. When dough has doubled in bulk, punch it down, divide in 4 pieces and shape into thin flat rounds. Let rise again while you prepare toppings.

Preheat oven to 375°F (190°C). If you have a pizza stone, put it on the bottom rack of the oven to heat. Line several pizza trays with parchment and lightly dust each with cornmeal. Evenly distribute toppings on each round in the order listed. The important thing is to add the crème fraiche and cheese at the end. Drizzle each pizza with oil, then sprinkle with salt and pepper. Bake for 20 to 25 minutes, or until crusty and golden. Serve hot.

● ● ● ●

MAKES 4, 10" (25 CM) ROUND PIZZAS

Recipe by dee Hobsbawn-Smith
Photography: Brian Gould

Pair With:
• Pinot Grigio
• B.C. Pinot Blanc
• South African Sauvignon Blanc

T acos Dorado

Pitillal Tomato Sauce:
6-8 Roma tomatoes
2 large garlic cloves
1 small white onion, sliced
1 jalapeño pepper, thinly sliced
1 tsp (5 mL) salt
4 cups (1 L) water

Filling:
2 cups (500 mL) cooked mashed
  potatoes
1 cup (250 mL) cooked, shredded
  chicken
3/4 cup (175 mL) grated mozzarella
3/4 cup (175 mL) Pitellal Tomato
  Sauce

20, 4" (10 cm) diameter white corn tortillas
1 cup (250 mL) lettuce OR cabbage, shredded
2 large tomatoes, sliced
1/2 cup (125 ml) diced sweet onion
1/2 cup (125 mL) sour cream
1/2 cup (125 mL) crumbled feta cheese
oil for frying

● ● ● ●

Sauce: Place all ingredients in a large saucepan over medium-high heat; bring to a boil. When tomatoes split, remove from heat. Strain the mixture through a sieve placed over a large bowl to reserve the juices. Place the tomato mixture in a blender and add salt to taste. Blend until smooth, adding reserved juices to thin the sauce to desired consistency.

Filling: Combine potatoes, chicken, mozzarella, and 1/2 cup (125 mL) sauce. Set aside.

Tacos: Place 1 tbsp (15 mL) filling on lower third of a tortilla and roll into a cigar shape. Place rolled tortillas seam-side down on a baking sheet. Prepare remaining tacos. Heat 1/2" (1.3 cm) oil in a skillet over medium-high heat. Place several tacos in pan, seam side down, and fry until golden and crispy, 5 to 8 minutes. Keep prepared tacos in warm oven.

Place cooked tacos on a plate and top with shredded lettuce or cabbage, tomatoes, onions and crumbled feta. Drizzle with sour cream and top with tomato sauce.

● ● ● ●

SERVES 5

Recipe by of Miriam Zolkewich
Photography: Brian Gould

Pair With:
● Corona Extra Beer
● Dos Equis amber Beer
● El Jimador Tequila Responsado

 rilled Maple-Ginger Marinated Steelhead Trout Burger with Ponzu Mayo

This citrus ginger sauce is a fabulous complement to the fresh trout burger.

2 tbsp (30 mL) maple syrup
2 tsp (10 mL) lime juice
1 tbsp (15 mL) finely grated fresh ginger
2, 6 oz (175 g) steelhead trout fillets, boneless, skinless
1/3 cup (75 mL) mayonnaise
1 tbsp plus 1 tsp (20 mL) ponzu*
1 French baguette
1/4 red onion, julienned
1/4 red pepper, julienned
4 pieces of butter leaf OR Boston lettuce

• • • •

In a shallow dish, combine maple syrup, lime juice and grated fresh ginger; add trout and marinate for 30 minutes.

In a small bowl, combine mayonnaise and ponzu; refrigerate until ready to use.

Preheat barbecue. Grill trout on hot grill about 7 to 8 minutes. Toast baguette on grill and spread with ponzu mayo. Top with trout fillet, julienned vegetables and lettuce.

* **Ponzu**: Available at Asian specialty stores, you can also make your own ponzu by combining: 1/3 cup (75 mL) soy sauce with 1 tbsp (15 mL) each grapefruit juice, lime juice, orange juice and rice wine vinegar. Stir in 2 tsp (10 mL) minced ginger.

• • • •

SERVES 2

Recipe by chef Curtis Toth

Photography: Patricia Holdsworth

Pair With:
• B.C. Sauvignon Blanc
• Oregon Pinot Gris
• Italian Pinot Grigio

Caramelized Pear, Camembert, Bacon & Toasted Walnut Sandwich

2 slightly ripe red pears
2 tbsp (30 mL) butter
1 small round Camembert cheese
4 thick slices pumpernickel bread, toasted
4 slices cooked bacon
2 oz (60 g) chopped walnuts, lightly toasted, divided
honey mustard

● ● ● ●

Cut pears in half vertically and core. Using a mandolin, cut pear halves into long slices, approximately 1/4" (6 mm) thick. In a skillet, melt butter over medium-high heat. Add pears and fry until brown on one side; flip and repeat. Remove pears and reserve. Cut enough cheese into 1/4" (6 mm) slices to cover 2 slices of toast. On 2 slices of toast, layer cheese, walnuts, pears and 2 bacon strips. Spread honey mustard on one side of remaining toast slices and place on top of bacon. Heat in oven or microwave until cheese begins to melt. Serve immediately.

● ● ● ●

MAKES 2 SANDWICHES

Recipe by Brandon Boone
Photography: Brian Gould

Pair With:
• Nut Brown Ale
• South of France Rosé
• Amontillado Sherry

Fig, Goat Cheese & Hot Capicolla Sandwich

4 thick slices focaccia
fig jam OR fig preserves*
1 small package of goat cheese, chilled then cut into 1/4" (6 mm) discs
4 oz (125 g) hot capicolla
2 ripe Roma tomatoes, sliced
salt and pepper, to taste
mixed salad greens

● ○ ○ ○

Toast focaccia slices. Spread fig jam on 2 pieces of toast. Top each with thin slices of goat cheese, capicolla and tomato slices. Season tomato with salt and pepper and top with salad greens. Finish each sandwich by placing 1 slice of remaining toast on top of greens. Slice on the bias and serve immediately.

* You can substitute fresh figs sliced vertically and drizzled with honey.

● ○ ○ ○

MAKES 2 SANDWICHES

Recipe by Brandon Boone
Photography: Brian Gould

Pair With:
● Pinot Grigio
● B.C. Pinot Blanc
● Alsatian Pinot Gris

Croque Madame Sandwiches with Sautéed Pears

6 tbsp (90 mL) unsalted butter
6 tbsp (90 mL) sugar
4 Anjou pears, peeled, cored, sliced
2 tbsp (30 mL) butter
8, 3/4" (2 cm) slices French bread
8 slices mortadella*
6 oz (170 g) grated old white Cheddar cheese
4 small eggs

• • • •

Preheat broiler. Melt butter in a large skillet over medium-high heat. Stir in sugar. Add pears and sauté until tender and golden, about 5 minutes. Cover and let stand at room temperature.

Preheat a large non-stick skillet over medium heat. Butter all bread slices on one side. Place buttered side down in skillet and cook until browned. Flip each slice and cook on the other side. Remove from heat. On the unbuttered side of each of 4 slices of toast, place sautéed pears in a single row and top with 2 slices of mortadella in a single row.

With the remaining 4 slices of toast, using a 2 1/2" (6 cm) diameter cookie cutter, cut a circle in the centre of each slice. Reserve toast circles. Place unbuttered side on top of mortadella and press firmly to compact. The toast has to be touching the mortadella evenly, so when the egg is added, it remains contained in the circle.

On a baking sheet, place all 4 sandwiches and the toast rounds. Sprinkle rounds with cheese. In each of the holes, break an egg. Sprinkle eggs lightly with cheese. Using aluminum foil, cover edges of toast so broiler will not burn toast. In oven, broil approximately 6" (15 cm) from broiler until egg white sets and the yolk is still very runny. Serve sandwiches with the cheese-topped toast round just barely covering the egg.

* Mortadella, a sausage from Bologna, Italy, is made from ground beef, pork, pork fat and seasonings.

• • • •

SERVES 4

Recipe by Brandon Boone
Photography: Brian Gould

Grilled Citrus Chicken Sandwich

Start these sandwiches a few hours in advance or up to one day before serving.

3 skinless boneless chicken breast halves
1/2 cup (125 mL) extra-virgin olive oil, divided
1/4 cup (60 mL) fresh lemon juice, divided
2 tbsp (30 mL) orange juice
1 tsp (5 mL) brown sugar
2 tsp (10 mL) dried herbes de Provence
4 garlic cloves, minced
salt and pepper, to taste
1 tsp (5 mL) anchovy paste
1 round sourdough bread loaf
7-8 fresh basil leaves
1 large tomato, thinly sliced
1/2 small red onion, thinly sliced
2 large romaine lettuce leaves

● ● ● ●

Using a meat mallet, pound chicken breasts between sheets of plastic wrap to 3/4" (2 cm) thickness. Combine 1/4 cup (60 mL) oil, 2 tbsp (30 mL) lemon juice, orange juice, sugar, herbes de Provence and half of garlic in a large resealable plastic bag. Add chicken to bag; shake to coat with marinade. Chill at least 2 hours and up to 6 hours.

Preheat barbecue to medium-high heat. Remove chicken from marinade and shake off any excess. Season chicken with salt and pepper. Grill chicken until cooked, approximately 4 minutes per side. Cool. Cut chicken on the bias into 1/2" (1.3 cm) thick slices. Combine anchovy paste, remaining lemon juice and garlic in a small bowl. Slowly whisk in remaining oil. Season dressing to taste with salt and pepper.

Cut bread loaf in half horizontally. Remove some of the soft interior from top half, leaving 1/2" (1.3 cm) thick shell; drizzle dressing evenly over inside of top and bottom of loaf. Fill sandwich with chicken and remaining ingredients. Replace top and wrap in plastic wrap. Slice sandwich into wedges before serving. This sandwich can be made 1 day ahead and refrigerated.

● ● ● ●

MAKES 4 SERVINGS

Recipe by Brandon Boone
Photography: Brian Gould

uffaletta Sandwich

Olive salad makes New Orleans' version of the Hero Sandwich outrageously good.

Olive Salad:
1/2 cup (125 mL) pitted, chopped black olives
1/2 cup (125 mL) chopped green olives stuffed with pimientos
1/2 cup (125 mL) chopped roasted red bell peppers
1/4 cup (60 mL) olive oil
3 tbsp (45 mL) chopped fresh flat-leaf parsley
1 tbsp (15 mL) finely chopped celery
3 garlic cloves, minced
1 tbsp (15 mL) white wine vinegar
salt and black pepper, to taste

Muffaletta:
1 round loaf Italian OR sourdough
   bread, approximately 10" (20 cm)
4 oz (125 g) mortadella*, thinly sliced
4 oz (125 g) cured Italian ham, such as
   prosciutto, thinly sliced
4 oz (125 g) Genoa salami, thinly sliced
4 oz (125 g) mozzarella cheese, sliced
4 oz (125 g) provolone cheese, sliced

● ● ● ●

Salad: Combine all ingredients in a bowl.
Marinate 2 to 3 hours at room temperature or cover and refrigerate for 24 hours. If refrigerated, bring to room temperature before making the muffaletta.

Muffaletta: Cut bread in half horizontally. Remove some of the centre to make room for filling. Spread about 1/4 cup (60 mL) of olive salad in the bottom portion of the bread. Layer meats alternately with layers of cheese. Top with additional olive salad and the top portion of the bread. Wrap muffaletta in plastic wrap and weigh down (a baking pan topped with a couple of cans will work) for approximately 30 minutes, Slice into wedges before serving.

Leftover olive salad can be added to pasta, rice or omelettes, used as dressing on a salad or as a spread for crackers or baguette slices.

* Mortadella, a sausage from Bologna, Italy, is made from ground beef, pork, pork fat and seasonings.

● ● ● ●

MAKES 4 LARGE WEDGES

Recipe by Claudine Gervais
Photography: Brian Gould

Pair With:
• Dolcetto D'alba
• Cotes De Ventoux Rose
• Pastis

hole Lotta Mojo Melt

Mojo Sauce:
3 tbsp (45 mL) olive oil
4 garlic cloves, finely minced
1 cup (250 mL) fresh orange juice
1/2 cup (125 mL) fresh lime juice
3/4 tsp (4 mL) ground cumin
salt and pepper, to taste

Sandwich:
1 tbsp (15 mL) butter
1 tbsp (15 mL) olive oil
6 oz (170 g) mixed brown and white mushrooms, sliced
1 French baguette, ends cut off, sliced in half and toasted
6 oz (175 g) Edam cheese
6 oz (175 g) honey ham, thinly sliced
6 oz (175 g) smoked turkey, thinly sliced
2 Roma tomatoes, thinly sliced

● ○ ● ○

Sauce: Heat oil in a skillet over medium-low heat. Add garlic and cook until lightly golden in colour. Strain oil into a bowl, discarding garlic; add juices and cumin. Season sauce with salt and pepper; cover and chill.

Sandwich: Heat butter and oil in a skillet over medium heat. Add mushrooms and sauté until browned. Remove from heat. Layer 1 baguette half with cheese slices, ham, turkey, mushrooms and tomatoes and top with remaining baguette slice. Heat in oven or microwave until cheese begins to melt. Cut into 2 pieces and serve with Mojo Sauce in a ramekin on the side for dipping.

● ○ ● ○

MAKES 2 SANDWICHES

Recipe by Brandon Boone

Photography: Brian Gould

Pair With:
• B.C. Sauvignon Blanc
• California Meritage
• White Bordeaux

Deluxe Hamburger with Herbed Goat Cheese & Grilled Watermelon

Deluxe Mayonnaise:
2 tbsp (30 mL) mayonnaise
1 tbsp (15 mL) EACH, ketchup and barbecue sauce

Herbed Goat Cheese:
1 tsp (5 mL) EACH, chopped fresh basil and thyme
1/2 tsp (2 mL) EACH, chopped fresh marjoram, chives and
    parsley
6, 1/4" (6 mm) slices of goat cheese

Hamburger:
2 tbsp (30 mL) Worcestershire sauce
1/4 cup (60 mL) diced white onion
2 tsp (10 mL) EACH, kosher salt and coarsely ground pepper
1 tbsp (15 mL) chopped fresh parsley
2 tbsp (30 mL) steak sauce (such as HP)
1 egg
2 lbs (1 kg) lean ground beef

6, 3/4" (2 cm) thick watermelon wedges
vegetable oil
6 kaiser buns, toasted
lettuce
ripe tomato, sliced
red onion, sliced
kosher dill pickles, sliced

● ○ ● ○

Mayonnaise: Combine all ingredients. Cover and refrigerate until ready to use.

Cheese: Mix all herbs together; roll each slice of goat cheese in herb mixture.

Hamburger: Combine all ingredients, except beef, in a bowl; mix well. Using your hands, gently fold in beef, handling as little as possible. Divide mixture into 6 balls on a waxed paper-lined cookie sheet. Gently press each ball until patties are about 4" (10 cm) in diameter. Cover patties with plastic wrap and chill overnight, if possible, or at least 4 to 6 hours before using. Preheat a barbecue. Cook patties over medium heat for 3 to 4 minutes each side (try to turn only once). Check patties for doneness by piercing with a fork. If juices run clear, remove from heat. Move patties to a cooler part of grill if they are getting too dark before being cooked through.

Brush watermelon slices with oil and grill for 1 minute each side.

Spread mayonaise on kaiser buns. Place a patty on each bun; top with goat cheese and grilled watermelon. Add remaining toppings as desired.

● ○ ● ○

SERVES 6

Recipe by chef Gregory Walsh

Photography: Hamid Attie Photography

Pair With:
• California Zinfandel
• Washington State Syrah
• Chilean Cabernet Sauvignon

APPETIZERS
....Starters and Snacks

Tuscan Spicy Oil with Artisan Bread

1 cup (250 mL) extra-virgin olive oil
1 tbsp (15 mL) paprika
1 tbsp (15 mL) hot chile flakes
1 large garlic clove, peeled
1 sprig rosemary
1/2 tsp (2 mL) kosher OR sea salt
1 tbsp (15 mL) balsamic vinegar
1 tbsp (15 mL) chopped fresh parsley
1 tbsp (15 mL) freshly grated Parmesan cheese

● ● ● ● ●

In a saucepan over medium-high heat, combine oil, paprika, chile flakes, garlic and rosemary; bring to a boil then reduce to low heat and simmer for 10 minutes. Remove from heat and let cool for 30 minutes. Once cool, add salt. Strain the oil into a sterile jar. Cover and refrigerate for up to two weeks.

When ready to serve, pour a 1/4 cup (60 mL) oil into a small dish; add balsamic vinegar, parsley and Parmesan. Serve with chunks of your favourite artisan bread.

● ● ● ● ●

MAKES 1 CUP / 250 ML OIL

Recipe by Brandon Boone
Photography: Brian Gould

Pair With:
• Sparkling Mineral Water
• Orange Vermouth
• Orvieto

Spicy Biscotti with Sun-Dried Tomatoes & Provolone

For those who like it hot, these biscotti pack punch! The most flavourful sun-dried tomatoes are soft and packed in oil; however, if all you have are the dry-pack variety, rehydrate by soaking in a bit of boiling water; then drain.

2 cups (500 mL) all-purpose flour
1 1/2 tsp (7 mL) baking powder
1/2 tsp (2 mL) salt
1/2 tsp (2 mL) crushed chile flakes
1/2 tsp (2 mL) dried oregano
1 cup (250 mL) grated provolone cheese
1 cup (250 mL) chopped almonds, divided
2 large eggs
1/3 cup (75 mL) dry white wine
1/4 cup (60 mL) olive oil OR oil from sun-dried tomatoes
3 sun-dried tomatoes, finely minced
1/2 tsp (2 mL) coarse salt

● ● ● ●

Preheat oven to 350°F (180°C). Line a large cookie sheet with aluminum foil or parchment paper. Stir flour with baking powder, salt, chile flakes and oregano; mix in provolone and 3/4 cup (175 mL) almonds. Set aside remaining almonds.

In a separate bowl, lightly beat eggs with wine; mix in oil and tomatoes. Stir into flour mixture until dough is evenly moistened. Using a rubber spatula, make a loaf of dough about 12" (30 cm) long. Wet hands and flatten loaf until about 3/4" (2 cm) thick. Sprinkle top with remaining almonds and coarse salt; lightly pat into dough.

Bake for 25 to 30 minutes, or until small cracks appear and loaf is firm to the touch. Grasping foil, slide loaf onto a large cutting board. Cut crosswise into 3/4" (2 cm) thick slices. Stand biscotti on baked edge about 1" (2.5 cm) apart on baking tray.

Reduce oven temperature to 325°F (160°C). Bake 25 minutes; then turn off oven. Leave biscotti in oven for 1 hour as it cools. Biscotti will feel quite dry to the touch. Store in an airtight container for several days or freeze for weeks.

● ● ● ●

MAKES 24

Recipe by Marilyn Bentz Crowley
Photography: Brian Gould

Pair With:
• Hunter Valley Semillon
• California Sang
• Chianti

Rye 'n' Swiss Biscotti with Black Onion Seed

Tiny triangular black onion seeds (nigella seeds), have a pleasant pungency. They are commonly available at health food, Indian and Middle Eastern stores.

1 cup (250 mL) EACH, all-purpose flour and rye flour
3 tsp (15 mL) black onion seeds, divided
2 tsp (10 mL) baking powder
1/2 tsp (2 mL) salt
3/4 cup (175 mL) grated Swiss Emmental OR Gruyère cheese
1/4 cup (60 mL) finely snipped chives OR thinly sliced green onion
2 large eggs
1/3 cup (75 mL) dry white wine
1/4 cup (60 mL) melted butter
1/2 tsp (2 mL) coarse salt

Preheat oven to 350°F (180°C). Line a large cookie sheet with aluminum foil or parchment paper. Stir flours with 2 tsp (10 mL) onion seeds, baking powder and salt; mix in cheese and chives. In a separate bowl, lightly beat eggs with wine. Stir into flour mixture along with melted butter until dough is evenly moistened. Using a rubber spatula, make a loaf of dough about 12" (30 cm) long. Wet hands and flatten loaf until about 3/4" (2 cm) thick. Sprinkle top with remaining 1 tsp (5 mL) onion seeds and coarse salt; lightly pat into dough.

Bake for 25 to 30 minutes, or until small cracks appear and loaf is firm to the touch. Grasping foil, slide loaf onto a large cutting board. Cut crosswise into 3/4" (2 cm) thick slices. Stand biscotti on baked edge about 1" (2.5 cm) apart on baking tray. Reduce oven temperature to 325°F (160°C). Bake 25 minutes; then turn off oven. Leave biscotti in oven for 1 hour as it cools. Biscotti will feel quite dry to the touch. Store in an airtight container for several days or freeze for weeks.

MAKES 24

Recipe by Marilyn Bentz Crowley
Photography: Brian Gould

Pair With:
• Stout Beer
• Canadian Whisky
• Fino Sherry

(G)ourmet Stuffed-Olive Sampler

Colossal Green Olives stuffed with Toasted Almond Slivers:
12-24 almond slivers
12 whole pitted colossal green olives

● ○ ○ ●

In a non-stick sauté pan over medium-low heat, toast almond slivers until lightly browned and fragrant. Remove from heat and let cool. Depending on size of olives, insert 1 or 2 almond slivers into each.

● ○ ○ ●

Colossal Green Olives stuffed with Chipotle Peppers:
1 can chipotle peppers in adobo sauce
12 whole pitted colossal green olives

● ○ ○ ●

Remove 2 or 3 large chipotle peppers from can and rinse under cold water; pat dry. Cut peppers into roughly the same depth and width as olive openings; stuff into olives. Keep refrigerated until ready to serve.

● ○ ○ ●

Colossal Green Olives stuffed with Cambozola:
1 small wedge of Cambozola cheese
12 whole pitted colossal green olives

● ○ ○ ●

Crumble cheese into a bowl. Using the thick end of a chopstick, stuff olives with cheese. Keep refrigerated until ready to serve.

● ○ ○ ●

Recipes by Brandon Boone
Photography: Brian Gould

Sun-dried Tomato, Snow Pea & Gouda Skewers

Simple, with sensational flavour and presentation.

1 jar whole sun-dried tomatoes
1 package whole snow peas
16 oz (500 g) pkg peppercorn Gouda
bamboo skewers
salt and pepper, to taste

● ● ● ●

Remove tomatoes from jar and drain in a bowl lined with paper towels. Cut into bite-sized pieces. Trim ends from snow peas and cut in half. Cube cheese into 1" (2.5 cm) cubes.

Using a bamboo skewer, pierce 1 whole sun-dried tomato, 4 snow pea halves and a cube of cheese, making sure not to pierce the cheese all the way through since it will be the base allowing your masterpiece to be presented standing up. To finish up, a shot of salt and a dusting of pepper and you're ready to go.

● ● ● ●

MAKES 8 SKEWERS

Recipe by Brandon Boone
Photography: Brian Gould

oney & Canadian Whisky Baked Figs

1/4 cup (60 mL) whole hazelnuts
1/4 cup (60 mL) slivered almonds
1/4 cup (60 mL) honey
1/4 cup (60 mL) Canadian whisky (such as Gibson's Finest)
1 1/2 tbsp (22 mL) butter
8 large or 12 small Mission figs, stemmed and cut in half
mint sprigs for garnish (optional)

● ○ ○ ○

Preheat oven to 450°F (230°C).

In a skillet over medium-low heat, toast hazelnuts and almonds until lightly browned. In a small saucepan, bring honey and whisky to a boil; remove from heat and reserve.

Coat the bottom of an ovenproof pan with butter. Lay figs, sliced side up, in a single layer. Drizzle with honey-whisky mixture. Sprinkle with hazelnuts and almonds.

Bake 7 to 10 minutes, or until softened. Remove from oven and cool until warm. Baste with pan juices, garnish with mint and serve immediately.

● ○ ○ ○

SERVES 4 AS AN APPETIZER

Recipe by Brandon Boone
Photography: Brian Gould

Pair With:
• Canadian Whisky
• Tawny Port
• Cava

Dino's Bruschetta

3 cups (750 mL) diced fresh tomatoes
1 tsp (5 mL) salt
2 tsp (10 mL) chopped fresh oregano
1/2 tsp (2 mL) pepper
1 1/2 tsp (7 mL) chopped garlic
1/2 cup (125 mL) extra-virgin olive oil, divided
1 tsp (5 mL) chile flakes
2 tsp (10 mL) EACH, chopped fresh basil and parsley
1 loaf of French bread OR baguette, sliced into 1" (2.5 cm) pieces
garlic cloves
butter

● ◦ ◦ ◦

Place tomatoes in a strainer and refrigerate overnight to drain. In a large bowl, combine tomatoes, salt, oregano and pepper. In a sauté pan over medium heat cook garlic, oil and chile flakes until garlic turns golden brown. Remove from heat and let cool to room temperature. Add garlic mixture to tomato mixture and stir well. Add basil and parsley and mix again. Briefly toast bread slices. Rub a small amount of fresh garlic on toast and spread with a little butter. Spoon tomato mixture onto toast and serve immediately.

● ◦ ◦ ◦

SERVES 8

Recipe by Dino Petrillo
Photography: John Ulan/Epic Photography

Pair With:
• Italian Pinot Grigio
• German Troken Riesling
• B.C. Gewürztraminar

White Bean & Rosemary Spread

Great on focaccia with grilled veggies.

1/4 cup plus 1 tbsp (75 mL) olive oil
1 tbsp (15 mL) butter
1 small onion, diced
1 tbsp (15 mL) minced garlic
pinch of red chile flakes
1 cup (250 g) canned white navy beans
1 large sprig fresh rosemary
1 bay leaf
4 cups (1 L) water
salt and pepper, to taste

● ● ● ●

Combine 1 tbsp (15 mL) oil and butter in a skillet over medium heat; add onion and sauté until just starting to brown. Add garlic and chiles; sauté 1 minute.

Add beans, rosemary, bay leaf and water. Bring to a boil, then simmer until beans are very soft. Drain off any unabsorbed water. Remove rosemary stem and bay leaf. Whisk beans while drizzling in olive oil (this will partly mash the beans). Add salt and pepper to taste.

● ● ● ●

Recipe by chef Alex Svenne
Photography: Brian Gould

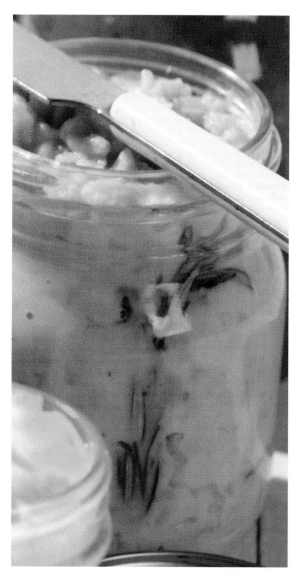

Grilled Vegetable Platter with Aïoli Dipping Sauce

This platter with garlicky Aïoli Dipping Sauce is an exceptional alternative to the ubiquitous cold vegetable crudités. You can adjust quantities according to the number of guests anticipated.

Aïoli Dipping Sauce:
1 slice white bread, crust removed
1/4 cup (60 mL) milk or enough to soak bread
4 garlic cloves, peeled and crushed
1 egg yolk
2 tbsp (30 mL) fresh lemon juice
1/2-3/4 cup (125-175 mL) olive oil
salt and freshly ground black pepper

Vegetables:
carrots, cut into sticks
celery sticks
sweet potatoes, parboiled and cut into wedges
red peppers, cut into 1" (2.5 cm) strips
green onions
olive oil to coat vegetables
salt and freshly ground black pepper

Sauce: In a small bowl, soak bread in milk, about 5 minutes. Squeeze milk from bread; combine bread, garlic, egg yolk and lemon juice in a blender or food processor. Process until smooth. With machine running, slowly drizzle in oil until mixture has thickened. Season with salt and pepper to taste. Refrigerate until ready to use.

Vegetables: In a large bowl, toss vegetables with 2 1/2 tbsp (37 mL) oil, or enough to coat. Season with salt and pepper. In a cast-iron grill pan or using an indoor grill over medium-high heat, grill vegetables until they are fork tender.

Arrange grilled vegetables on a serving platter. Serve warm with Aïoli Dipping Sauce.

Recipe by Claudine Gervais
Photography: Brian Gould

Pair With:
• California Zinfandel
• Rioja Rose
• Australian Viognier

Homemade Herbed Chèvre Spread with Grilled Crostini

Herbed Chèvre Spread:
11 oz (300 g) creamy goat cheese,
   at room temperature
3/4 cup (175 mL) whipping cream
1 medium garlic clove, minced
2 1/2 tbsp (37 mL) finely chopped
   mixed herbs such as basil, thyme,
   oregano and parsley
2 1/2 tbsp (37 mL) finely snipped
   chives OR thinly sliced green onion
1/2 tsp (2 mL) freshly ground black
   pepper
1/4 tsp (1 mL) salt

Crostini:
2 day-old baguettes
1/4 cup (60 mL) olive oil
1 large garlic clove, crushed

● ● ● ●

Herbed Chèvre Spread: Using a wooden spoon, break up cheese in a mixing bowl. Slowly stir in cream, mixing well between additions. When smooth, add remaining ingredients, stirring well. Scoop into a serving crock, sprinkle with additional chopped herbs and serve with crostini, whole-wheat pita crisps or crackers. Covered and refrigerated, this cheese spread mellows and keeps well for several days. Makes 2 cups.

Crostini: Cut baguettes into 1/4" (6 mm) slices. In a small pot over medium-low heat, heat oil. When warmed, add garlic; turn off heat and let sit for 10 minutes. Drain oil into a small bowl, discarding garlic. Brush garlic oil on one side of baguette slices. Grill oiled side of baguette slices on a barbecue until lightly charred. Serve warm with cheese spread.

● ● ● ●

SERVES 6

Recipe by Marilyn Bentz Crowley
Photography: Brian Gould

Pair With:
• White Bordeaux
• B.C. Zweigelt
• Côtes de Provence Rosé

Roasted Red Pepper, Walnut & Feta Dip
with Salt & Pepper Pita Chips

4-5 red bell peppers
2 tbsp (15 mL) olive oil, divided
2 shallots, chopped
1/2 cup (125 mL) chopped,
    toasted walnuts
1 tbsp (15 mL) ground cumin
1/2 tsp (2 mL) ancho chile powder
    OR cayenne
1 head garlic, roasted
1 tsp (5 mL) honey
1 tsp (5 mL) kosher salt
1/2 cup (125 mL) feta cheese

Salt & Pepper Pita Chips:
4 pitas
2 tbsp (30 mL) olive oil
1 tsp (5 mL) dried parsley
2 tsp (10 mL) sea salt
2 tsp (10 mL) coarsely ground
    black pepper

● ● ● ●

Using a pastry brush, baste peppers with 1 tbsp (15 mL) oil. Char peppers directly over a gas flame or under a broiler, until blackened on all sides. Place peppers in a plastic sandwich bag or brown paper bag for 15 minutes. Peel, seed and cut peppers into slices. Heat remaining oil in a skillet over medium heat; add shallots and sauté until golden. Add walnuts, cumin, chile powder, garlic, honey and salt; mix well. Remove from heat and let cool. In a food processor, combine peppers, shallot mixture and feta cheese; process until smooth. Cover and chill until ready to use. Serve at room temperature.

Chips: Preheat oven to 400°F (200°C). Cut each pita into 8 wedges. Arrange the wedges on a large baking sheet. Brush with olive oil then sprinkle with parsley, salt and pepper. Bake for approximately 8 minutes, or until golden. Remove from oven and let cool. Store in an airtight container until ready to use.

● ● ● ●

Recipe by Brandon Boone
Photography: Brian Gould

Pair With:
• Vihno Verde
• Austrian Gruener Veltliner
• Verdicchio

Triple-Cream Brie with Prosciutto & Honey-Roasted Peaches

Silky Brie, salty prosciutto and sweet peaches – superb.

2 peaches, pitted and cut into 4 wedges each
1/4 cup (60 mL) honey
1/2 cup (125 mL) balsamic vinegar
small wheel triple-cream Brie, cut into 8 wedges
8 slices of prosciutto

● ○ ○ ○

Preheat oven to 350°F (180°C). Toss peach wedges with honey. Place on a rimmed baking sheet and bake in oven until soft and honey is starting to brown, approximately 20 minutes. Remove from oven and let cool to room temperature, reserving honey/juice left in pan. In a small saucepan over medium-high heat, boil balsamic vinegar and reduce to 1/4 cup (60 mL). Remove from heat and let cool.

Wrap each piece of brie with a slice of prosciutto and top with a peach wedge. Drizzle reserved honey mixture around Brie, then drizzle with balsamic reduction.

● ○ ○ ○

SERVES 4 AS AN APPETIZER

Recipe by chef Alex Svenne

Photography: Brian Gould

Pair With:
• California Sauvignon Blanc
• South African Chenin Blanc
• Alsace Pinot Gris

Port-infused Camembert with Hot Pepper Sauce & Toasted Almonds

A fabulous campfire appetizer, but you can make it year-round on the barbecue or in the oven.

2, 4 oz (115 g) rounds of Camembert
1/4 cup (60 mL) ruby port
1/3 cup (75 mL) sweet chili sauce OR good-quality roasted red pepper dip
1/4 cup (60 mL) toasted almonds

● ○ ○ ●

Place a large sheet of aluminum foil inside an aluminum pie plate or cast-iron skillet. Quarter Camembert rounds and arrange on foil sheet. Drizzle port over cheese. Spoon sweet chili sauce over cheese. Top with toasted almonds. Gather foil to make a loose package.

Place on medium-cool area of fire pit grill or barbecue or in 300°F (150°C) oven for 15 minutes, or until you can hear the cheese bubbling. Remove from heat. Lift aluminum foil packet from pie plate and place on serving dish. Carefully open packet. Serve with crostini or sturdy crackers.

● ○ ○ ●

SERVES 4 TO 6

Recipe by Shel Zolkewich
Photography: Brian Gould

Pair With:
• Hernder Estate Riesling VQA
• St. Hubertus Riesling VQA
• Bouvet Ladubay Sparkling Brut de Blanc

aganaki

This Greek flambéed cheese is a great-tasting quick appetizer!

1 tbsp (15 mL) olive oil
1/4 cup (60 mL) white flour
5 oz (140 g) kefalogravgiera cheese (sometimes referred to as saganaki cheese, but try to get kefalogravgiera)
1 tbsp (15 mL) brandy
1 fresh lemon wedge

• ○ ○ •

Heat oil in a skillet over medium-high heat. Lightly flour cheese on both sides and place in skillet. Fry cheese on both sides until light golden brown in colour but do not let cheese get too soft – it should still retain its shape.

Remove pan from heat; add brandy and flambé. Yell OPAH! and then squeeze lemon over cheese until flame is out. Remove from pan and serve.

• ○ ○ •

SERVES 2 AS AN APPETIZER

Recipe by Tony Katsabanis
Photography: Brian Gould

Pair With:
• Retsoma
• Australian Riesling
• B.C. Sauvignon Blanc

ⓢpanakopita

1/2 cup (125 mL) EACH,
   clarified butter* and
   olive oil
2 lbs (1 kg) baby spinach
12 green onions, chopped
1/2 cup (125 mL) bread
   crumbs
1/4 tsp (1 mL) white pepper
1/2 cup (125 mL) finely
   chopped fresh parsley
1/4 tsp (1 mL) minced fresh
   dill
3 eggs
12 oz (375 g) crumbled feta
   cheese
8 oz (250 g) kefalogravgiera
   cheese OR Parmesan
   cheese
12 oz (375 g) phyllo pastry
   dough

● ○ ○ ○

In a small bowl, whisk together butter and oil; reserve. In a large pot of boiling water, blanch spinach for 2 1/2 minutes; remove, let dry, then chop. In a skillet over medium heat, sauté onions in half of butter mixture for 4 minutes; add spinach and sauté for 5 minutes. Remove onions and spinach from heat; let cool until warm. Add bread crumbs, pepper, parsley, dill, eggs and cheeses; mix well. Set aside.

Using a pastry brush, grease a 9 x 15" (23 x 38 cm) baking pan with butter mixture. Put down 1 sheet of phyllo on pan and lightly brush with butter. Lay down another sheet of phyllo and brush with butter. Continue until you have 4 sheets of phyllo on the pan. Add spinach mixture and spread evenly over phyllo. Fold any phyllo overlapping the pan on top of spinach mixture. Continue adding phyllo sheets on top of the spinach, brushing between each sheet with butter until remaining phyllo is used. Cut into 3" (8 cm) squares. Bake at 325°F (160°C) for 35 minutes, or until golden brown.

* unsalted butter that has been melted and skimmed of milk solids

● ○ ○ ○

MAKES 15 PIECES

Recipe by George Katsabanis

Photography: Brian Gould

Pair With:
• Retsina
• Vihno Verde
• Pilsner

Teriyaki Beef Sushi

sirloin steak (enough to make 32 thin slices)
1/2 cup (125 mL) teriyaki sauce
1 tsp (5 mL) sesame oil
2 1/2 cups (625 mL) uncooked sushi rice
8 sheets nori (dried seaweed)
toasted sesame seeds

Place steak in freezer for 10 to 15 minutes to make it easier to slice. Remove when chilled and cut slices as thinly as possible. Mix teriyaki sauce and sesame oil; add steak and marinade for 30 minutes in refrigerator.

Meanwhile, cook sushi rice according to package directions. Cut nori sheets into quarters. Grill steak in a hot skillet, searing the outside while the inside remains medium-rare.

To Assemble: Spoon a small amount of rice diagonally across the centre of the nori. Sprinkle lightly with toasted sesame seeds. Lay a strip of teriyaki steak on the rice. Roll the nori tightly into a cone, moistening the edge to seal. Cover cones with plastic wrap and refrigerate up to 4 hours. Serve with soy sauce.

MAKES 32 SMALL CONES

Recipe by Brandon Boone
Photography: Brian Gould

(S)ushi, Squared

6 sheets dark green nori (dried seaweed)
1/4 cup (60 mL) mayonnaise
1 tsp (5 mL) wasabi paste
4 cups (1 L) prepared and seasoned sushi rice
8 oz (250 g) smoked salmon, thinly sliced
2 tbsp (30 mL) toasted sesame seeds
1/4 cup (60 mL) thinly sliced pickled ginger

● ● ● ●

Oil and line a 9 x 9" (23 x 23 cm) pan with plastic wrap. Lay a piece of nori, shiny side down, on top of plastic wrap, trimming the sheet to fit neatly in a single layer.

Mix mayonnaise and wasabi, reserve. Pat half the rice over nori layer, spreading it evenly to the edges. Spread rice layer with wasabi-mayo, adding more if you prefer it spicier. Lay salmon over the rice, trimming to fit (save any scraps for 'testing'). Top with a second layer of nori. Pat down. Top with the remaining rice. Sprinkle evenly with toasted sesame seeds. Distribute pickled ginger evenly over the entire surface. Cover with nori, shiny side up, pushing down lightly. Cover with plastic wrap, laying it directly on the nori. Place something heavy on top – a second cake pan weighted with a couple of 28 oz tins will do it. Refrigerate for at least 1 hour or up to 8 hours.

Using a sharp knife, dip the tip in water; let water drip down edge before cutting. Slice sushi into desired pattern. Wipe blade with a damp cloth and dip tip of knife into water after each cut.

● ● ● ●

MAKES 36 PIECES

Recipe by Brandon Boone
Photography: Brian Gould

(S)moked Salmon Tortilla Rolls

8 oz (250 g) cream cheese
1 tbsp (15 mL) chopped fresh dill OR 1 tsp (5 mL) dry dill
salt and pepper, to taste
4, 10" (25 cm) flour tortillas, such as pesto or spinach
1 lb (500 g) smoked salmon (lox), sliced
1 small jar of roasted red peppers OR capers (both optional)

● ● ● ●

In a food processor or electric mixer, whip cream cheese until soft. Add dill; adjust seasoning with salt and pepper. Spread tortilla shells with dill cream cheese.

Lay smoked salmon over cream cheese on tortilla. If you wish, lay a strip of capers or roasted peppers along tortilla.

Roll tortilla into a tight roll. Wrap with plastic wrap and refrigerate.

To serve, slice roll in 1/2" (1.25 cm) pinwheels.

● ● ● ●

Recipe by chef Alex Svenne
Photography: Brian Gould

Pair With:
• Gnangara Unwooded Chardonnay

Smoked Salmon Blini with Crème Fraîche, Chives & Fish Roe

Blini:
1 tbsp (7 g) active dry yeast
    (1 env)
pinch sugar
1/4 cup (60 mL) warm water
1 1/4 cups (300 mL) warm milk
4 eggs, separated
1 tsp (5 mL) salt
1 tsp (5 mL) sugar
1/4 cup (60 mL) unsalted butter,
    melted
2/3 cup (150 mL) cornmeal,
    finely ground in blender or
    food processor
1 1/3 cups (325 mL) unbleached
    all-purpose flour

crème fraîche
smoked salmon
fish roe
fresh dill
fresh chives

• • • •

In a small bowl, combine yeast, sugar and warm water; stir to dissolve. Let stand until foamy, approximately 10 minutes. Using an electric mixer, combine milk, egg yolks, salt, sugar, butter and yeast mixture until incorporated; add cornmeal and flour and continue to mix until mixture is smooth and the consistency of whipping cream. Cover with plastic wrap and let stand at room temperature until doubled, about 1 hour.

In a separate bowl, beat egg whites until firm peaks form; fold into reserved batter. Heat a skillet over medium heat; brush with melted butter. Spoon 1 tbsp (15 mL) of batter into hot pan; cook until bubbles break on surface, about 1 minute. Flip and repeat with remaining batter. Keep blini warm, covered with foil, in an oven set on low heat until ready to serve. Brush each blin with melted butter, if desired.

To Assemble: Spread 1 tsp (5 mL) crème fraîche on 1 blin; top with smoked salmon and 2 fronds of fresh dill; layer with a second blin. Using a pastry bag, squeeze crème fraîche on top and garnish with chives and a dollop of fish roe. Repeat with remaining blini.

• • • •

MAKES 60 TO 80 COCKTAIL-SIZED BLINI

Recipe by Claudine Gervais
Photography: Brian Gould

moked Goldeye with Swiss Chard & Cucumber Carrot Pickles

1 lb (500 g) smoked goldeye, skinned and filleted

Cucumber Carrot Pickles:
1 tbsp (15 mL) brown sugar
3 cups (750 mL) water
1/4 cup (60 mL) vinegar
1 English cucumber, sliced very thinly
1 medium carrot, sliced very thinly

2 lb (1 kg) Swiss chard
1 1/2 tbsp (22 mL) butter, divided
2 cloves crushed garlic

● ● ● ●

Prepare goldeye.

Pickles: Dissolve sugar in water. Add vinegar. Add vegetables to liquid and marinate in the fridge for at least 1 hour or up to 1 day. Drain liquid before garnishing goldeye.

Remove stems from Swiss chard and cut into 1/4" (6 mm) strips. Set aside. Tear or chop chard leaves into bite-sized pieces. Set aside. Melt 1 tbsp (15 mL) butter in a large sauté pan over medium heat. Add chard stems and garlic. Sauté 1 minute. Add remaining butter to pan; stir in chard leaves. Increase heat to medium-high and cook, stirring occasionally, 3 to 5 minutes, or until leaves are tender.

Divide chard mixture among 4 plates. Top with goldeye and garnish with Cucumber Carrot Pickles.

● ● ● ●

SERVES 4

Recipe by Cheryl Cohan
Photography: Brian Gould

Pair With:
• Prosecco
• Alsatian Pinot Gris
• Mosel Riesling Kabinett

Lake Trout Gravlax, Smoked Goldeye Mousse & Whitefish Caviar

Gravlax:
2 oz (60 mL) lemon juice
1 oz (30 mL) vodka or gin
1 boned trout fillet
1/2 cup (125 mL) kosher salt
2 tbsp (30 mL) coarse black
pepper
1/4 cup (60 mL) brown sugar
1/4 cup (60 mL) chopped fresh
dill or 2 tbsp (30 mL) dry dill

Smoked Goldeye Mousse:
1 smoked goldeye
8 oz (250 g) cream cheese
dash Worcestershire sauce
dash Tabasco

2 oz (60 mL) whitefish caviar for
garnish

Gravlax: Combine lemon juice and vodka. Brush trout with juice. Combine salt, pepper, sugar and dill. Spread evenly to coat trout fillet. Wrap trout in cheesecloth or a clean dishtowel. Place in a lasagne pan. Place a second pan on top as a weight. Cure in refrigerator for 3 days. To serve, brush off cure mix and slice thinly at an angle. Gravlax will keep in the fridge for up to a week or will freeze well.

Mousse: Remove goldeye skin and bones. Purée fish in food processor. Add cream cheese, Worcestershire and Tabasco. Purée until very smooth. Transfer to a piping bag and chill.

To Serve: Lay out a sheet of plastic wrap. Thinly slice gravlax and lay on plastic wrap in a 4" (10 cm) wide strip. Pipe a strip of goldeye mousse down centre of gravlax. Roll gravlax around goldeye. Wrap with plastic wrap and chill. Slice 1 1/2" (3.75 cm) pieces of gravlax roll and stand up on plate. Spoon 1 1/2 tsp (7 mL) of caviar on top of each roll. Serve with minced red onion, cucumber slices, sour cream, capers and crackers.

Recipe by chef Alex Svenne
Photography: Brian Gould

Pair With:
• Domaine Laroche Chablis Premier Cru

Wild Pike with Cranberry Dressing & Beet Salad Tapas

Beets:
2-3 medium beets
juice from 1/2 an orange
1 tsp (5 mL) olive oil
1 tsp (5 mL) balsamic vinegar
1 tsp (5 mL) chopped fresh dill

Cranberry Dressing:
1/2 cup (125 ml) cranberry juice
juice of 1 lemon (reserve some zest for garnish)
1/2 cup (125) vegetable oil
salt and pepper, to taste

1/4 cup (60 mL) whole peppercorns
1/4 cup (60 mL) coarse salt (do not use regular salt)
1/4 cup (60 mL) sesame seeds
1 lb (500 g) northern pike fillets OR other firm-fleshed fish
1 handful of mixed field greens
1 tbsp (30 mL) vegetable oil

● ● ● ●

Beets: Roast or boil beets until tender. Remove from heat and let cool. Remove skins, halve and slice. Toss with remaining ingredients.

Dressing: In a bowl, whisk together juices and oil. Season with salt and pepper.

In a spice grinder, grind peppercorns and coarse salt until they become a fine powder. Remove and combine with sesame seeds. Dust both sides of fillets with spice mixture and reserve. Heat oil in a large pan over medium-high heat. Sear fillet for 3 minutes; flip and sear for 1 minute. Remove from pan and cut into 4 portions.

Divide greens among 4 plates. Divide fish among the greens. Drizzle with Cranberry Dressing. Top with sliced beets and garnish with lemon zest. Serve immediately.

● ● ● ●

SERVES 4

Recipe by Cheryl Cohan

Pair With:
• White Burgundy
• B.C. Gewürztraminer
• California Viognier

Cayenne-Spiked Golden Calamari with Garlic & Lemon Aioli

Garlic & Lemon Aioli:
1/2 cup (125 mL) olive oil
2 large garlic cloves
juice and grated zest of 1 lemon
1 tsp (5 mL) Dijon mustard
pinch of cayenne
1 egg yolk
salt and pepper, to taste

Golden Calamari:
2 cups (500 mL) canola oil
1/2 cup (125 mL) flour
1 tbsp (15 mL) cornstarch
1 tsp (5 mL) paprika
1/2 tsp (2 mL) dry mustard
pinch of cayenne
20 small squid rings
sea salt, to taste

Aioli: In a saucepan, heat oil over medium-low heat. Add garlic and simmer until golden brown and soft; remove cloves, reserving oil. Let cool to room temperature. Mash garlic and mix with lemon juice, mustard, cayenne and egg yolk. Whisk yolk mixture and very slowly drizzle in olive oil, whisking until thickened to mayonnaise consistency. Stir in lemon zest and add salt and pepper as desired.

Calamari: Heat oil in small saucepan. Combine flour, cornstarch and spices. Toss squid in flour mixture. Deep-fry in oil for 45 seconds, until crisp and golden. Place on paper towels to drain and sprinkle with salt.

Divide calamari among 4 plates and serve with a dollop of aioli.

SERVES 4

Recipe by chef Alex Svenne
Photography: Brian Gould

Pair With:
• India Pale Ale
• B.C. Sauvignon Blanc
• Lager

Artichoke Bottoms Stuffed with Garlic Mushrooms & Shrimp Topped with Aged White Cheddar

12 frozen artichoke bottoms*
1 tbsp (15 mL) olive oil
1/4 cup (60 mL) butter
1 small onion, diced
1 cup (250 mL) sliced mushrooms
1 garlic clove, minced
12 large tiger shrimp
juice of 1/2 lemon
2 oz (60 mL) white wine OR white
   vermouth
1 small tomato, diced
1 tbsp (15 mL) chopped parsley
pinch of dried chile flakes
salt and pepper, to taste
4 oz (125 g) old white Cheddar,
   shredded

● ● ● ●

Preheat oven to 400°F (200°C).

Arrange artichoke bottoms in a greased lasagne pan. Heat oil and butter in a sauté pan over medium-high heat until melted. Add onion and sauté until translucent. Add mushrooms and garlic; sauté until mushrooms have browned and softened. Add shrimp and sauté until opaque. Add lemon juice and white wine; let reduce for 2 minutes. Add tomato, parsley and chile flakes; season with salt and pepper. Pile mushroom mixture into artichoke bottoms. Top with grated Cheddar. Bake until cheese is bubbly.

* available at specialty food markets. If unavailable, substitute fresh artichokes

● ● ● ●

Recipe by chef Alex Svenne
Photography: Brian Gould

Pair With:
• New Zealand Sauvignon Blanc
• Dry Provence Rosé

Chesapeake Shrimp with Fresh Tomato & Horseradish Dip

You can find Old Bay Seasoning at the fishmonger's and at large supermarkets.

Fresh Tomato & Horseradish Dip:
1 large lemon
1 cup (250 mL) very ripe grape OR cherry tomatoes
1/2 cup (125 mL) thick chili sauce OR ketchup
2 tbsp (30 mL) grated horseradish, squeezed dry
2 tbsp (30 mL) chopped fresh parsley

1/2 cup (125 mL) water
2 tbsp (30 mL) Old Bay Seasoning
1 lb (500 g) frozen or fresh shrimp in zipper-back shells

● ● ● ●

Dip: Grate lemon zest and squeeze juice; set aside. Cut tomatoes in half; squeeze out and discard seedy interior. In a blender, whirl tomatoes with chili sauce and 1 tbsp (15 mL) lemon juice. Briefly whirl in horseradish; turn into a small deep serving bowl. Garnish with pinches of parsley and lemon zest; set aside.

When ready to serve, bring water, Old Bay Seasoning and remaining lemon juice to a boil in a large saucepan over high heat. Add shrimp all at once; cover and return to a boil; this takes about 5 minutes with frozen shrimp, less with fresh. Stir shrimp and, when all are uniformly pink, immediately drain in a colander. Turn into a warmed serving bowl; scatter with remaining lemon zest and parsley. Serve immediately with dipping sauce and plenty of serviettes.

● ● ● ●

SERVES 4 TO 6 WITH A GENEROUS
1 CUP (250 ML) SAUCE

Recipe by Marilyn Bentz Crowley
Photography: Brian Gould

Pair With:
• Groner Veltliner
• Hungarian Pinot Gris
• B.C. Sauvignon Blanc

Lobster Nachos with Chipotle, Mâche & Asiago Cheese

2, 1/2 lb lobsters
1 tbsp (15 mL) butter
1 small onion, chopped
1 carrot, diced
1 celery stalk, chopped
2 chipotle peppers
1 tbsp (15 mL) tomato paste
1 tbsp (15 mL) rice
1/4 cup (60 mL) whipping cream
1 tbsp (15 mL) bourbon
    (substitute Scotch, rye
    whisky or even brandy)
1 lb (500 g) blue corn chips
1 cup (250 g) Asiago, thinly
    sliced (it will break into
    shards)
1/2 cup (125 mL) mâche leaves
    (corn salad) OR baby arugula

• • • •

When selecting lobsters, choose ones that are quite lively. Fill a large pot with water and add salt liberally. Bring to a full boil. Drop lobsters into water head first. Cook for 10 minutes. They will turn bright red. Plunge cooked lobsters into an ice-water bath. Crack shells and remove meat from lobster. Reserve claws for garnish.

Break up lobster shells. Heat butter in heavy pot. Cook lobster shells in butter for a few minutes to draw out flavour. Add onion, carrot and celery. Add enough water to cover. Bring to a simmer. Simmer for 45 minutes.

Strain liquid. Return liquid to pot, bring to a boil and reduce to 1 cup (250 mL). Add chipotle peppers, tomato paste and rice. Bring to a boil; cook till rice is soft. Purée. Add cream and bourbon. Cool.

On each of 4 ovenproof plates, place a small pile of corn chips. Top chips with 1/2 the lobster meat and 1/2 the Asiago. Bake at 350°F (180°C) until cheese is melted. Top with more chips, lobster and cheese. Bake again.

Top with mâche leaves and drizzle chipotle sauce on plates.

• • • •

Recipe by chef Alex Svenne
Photography: Brian Gould

Pair With:
• Gosset Grand Reserve NV Brut Champagne

Lobster & Shrimp Mousse

An exquisite appetizer from Fuller's time at the Paris Ritz Hotel.

Mousse:
1 1/2 lobster tails
3 oz (90 g) shrimp
6 tbsp (90 mL) lemon juice
2 tbsp (30 mL) brandy
1 3/4 cups (425 mL) whipping cream, divided
12 eggs, separated
1/4 cup (60 mL) chopped fresh dill
2 tbsp (30 mL) chopped fresh parsley
salt and pepper to taste

Sambuca-Tomato Hollandaise:
1/4 tsp (2 mL) EACH, crushed peppercorns and salt
3 tbsp (45 mL) white vinegar
2 tbsp (30 mL) cold water
6 egg yolks
2 1/4 cups (560 mL) butter, clarified, warm
1 1/2 tbsp (22 mL) lemon juice
2 tbsp (30 mL) tomato purée
1 tbsp (15 mL) sambuca
salt and pepper to taste

Mousse: Poach lobster in boiling salted water 4 minutes. In food processor, combine shrimp, lemon juice, brandy and 1 1/2 cups (375 mL) cream; blend well. Push shrimp through a sieve. Add yolks, remaining cream, dill and parsley. In a bowl, beat egg whites until stiff. Fold shrimp mixture into egg whites. Add salt and pepper to taste.

Divide mousse in 2 parts. Lay out 6 pieces of plastic wrap, 8 1/2 x 11" (21 x 28 cm). Spread mousse evenly on wrap, leaving 2" (5 cm) top and bottom and room on sides to tie once rolled. Cut lobster tail in quarters lengthwise. Place 1/4 of each tail horizontally in middle of mousse, leaving some tail hanging out on 1 side. Bring top of wrap down to bottom and roll into cigar shape. Tie ends as close to mousse as possible, making sure there is little or no air in the package. Poach in boiling water for 8 minutes. Refrigerate until cold. Unwrap, cut into disks and serve with Hollandaise.

Hollandaise: Combine peppercorns, salt and vinegar in a saucepan. Reduce, over medium heat, until nearly dry. Remove from heat and add cold water. Transfer to a stainless-steel bowl. Add egg yolks and beat well. Hold bowl over pot of hot water and beat until yolks are thick and creamy. Remove from heat. Using a ladle, slowly add butter, beating well. If sauce thickens too much before all butter is added, add some lemon juice. Once all butter has been added, whisk in tomato purée, sambuca and lemon juice. Season with salt and pepper to taste.

SERVES 6

Recipe by chef Rob Fuller

Photography: Patricia Holdsworth

Pair With:
• Pastis
• Vindo Verde
• India Pale Ale

Californian Grilled Chicken & Sun-dried Tomato Nachos

1 tbsp (15 mL) EACH, ketchup and soy sauce
2 tbsp (30 mL) canola oil
1/2 tsp (2 mL) black pepper
1 tbsp (15 mL) chopped basil or 1 tsp (5 mL) dried basil
1 tsp (5 mL) minced garlic
4 chicken breasts
1 lb (500 g) bag tortilla chips
1/4 cup (60 mL) sun-dried tomatoes, soaked and sliced
1 small red onion, sliced
1/2 cup (125 mL) sliced banana peppers OR jalapeños (optional)
1/2 cup (125 g) EACH, grated Cheddar and Monterey Jack cheese
1/2 cup (125 mL) shredded lettuce
1 cup (250 mL) diced tomatoes
1/2 cup (125 mL) sliced green onion
1/2 cup (125 mL) EACH, salsa and sour cream

● ● ● ●

Combine ketchup, soy sauce, oil, pepper, basil and garlic; add chicken. Marinate 30 minutes. Barbecue chicken or pan fry. Cook 3 minutes each side. Cool and slice.

Lay half the nacho chips on a pizza pan. Top with half the chicken, sun-dried tomatoes, red onion and hot peppers, if using. Sprinkle with half the cheese. Bake at 400°F (200°C) until cheese is melted. Top with remaining chicken, sun-dried tomato, onion, peppers and cheese. Return to oven until cheese is melted and bubbly.

Top with lettuce, tomatoes and green onions. Serve with salsa and sour cream.

● ● ● ●

Recipe by chef Alex Svenne
Photography: Brian Gould

Pair With:
• Deinhard Sparkling Lila

Grand Marnier Chicken Wings

Grand Marnier Marinade:
1/2 cup (125 mL) Grand Marnier
1/4 cup (60 mL) freshly squeezed lime juice
1/4 cup (60 mL) soy sauce
3 tbsp (45 mL) sweet chili chicken sauce*
1 tbsp (15 mL) orange zest
1" (2.5 cm) piece of fresh ginger, finely shredded
3 garlic cloves, minced
1 tsp (5 mL) kosher salt
1 tsp (5 mL) ground black pepper

2 lbs (1 kg) chicken wings or drumettes

● ○ ○ ○

Marinade: Combine marinade ingredients in a glass bowl and whisk well.

Place chicken in a resealable plastic bag or shallow baking dish and cover with marinade. Place in refrigerator and let stand at least 1/2 an hour up to overnight, stirring
occasionally.

Preheat oven to 425°F (220°C). Remove chicken from marinade before baking. Roast
chicken until juices run clear when pricked with a toothpick or fork, roughly 1 hour,
turning occasionally so wings can brown.

Drizzle cooked wings with additional sweet chili chicken sauce and serve.

* available in the Asian section at most supermarkets

● ○ ○ ○

SERVES 4

Recipe by Brandon Boone
Photography: Brian Gould

Pair With:
• Grey Monk Pinot Noir
• Rosemount Estate Chardonnay
• Cave Spring Sauvignon Blanc

ⒷÐraised Wild Mushrooms & Soba Noodles Tapas

1/2 lb (250 g) soba noodles
1 tsp (5 mL) sesame oil
salt and pepper, to taste
2 tbsp (30 mL) olive oil
1 tbsp (15 mL) butter
1/2 red onion, sliced
1 1/2 cups (750 mL) sliced wild mushrooms
2 garlic cloves, chopped
3 tbsp (45 mL) chopped fresh parsley, plus sprigs for garnish
2 tbsp (30 mL) dry white wine

● ● ● ●

In a pot of boiling water, cook soba noodles until al dente. Drain; toss with sesame oil. Season with salt and pepper.

Heat olive oil and butter in a skillet over medium-high heat. Add onion and sauté approximately 2 minutes. Reduce heat to medium and add mushrooms, garlic and parsley. Sauté 2 minutes, or until tender. Deglaze pan with wine and cook 3 to 5 minutes more. Drain off any excess liquid.

Place soba noodles on small plates and top with mushrooms. Garnish with parsley.

● ● ● ●

SERVES 4

Recipe by Cheryl Cohan
Photography: Brian Gould

Pair With:
• White Bordeaux
• Alsatian Gewürztraminer
• B.C. Pinot Blanc

Wild Mushroom Hors D'oeuvres

Cream Puffs:
1 cup (250 mL) water
4 oz (125 mL) butter, cut in
6 slices
1/4 tsp (1 mL) salt
1 cup (250 mL) flour
4 eggs

Mushroom Filling:
3 tbsp (45 mL) butter
8 oz (250 g) wild
mushrooms, sliced
1 medium white onion,
diced
1 tsp (5 mL) salt
1/4 tsp (1 mL) dried thyme
  or 1 tsp (5 mL) fresh
2 tbsp (30 mL) flour
1 cup (250 mL) sour cream

Cream Puffs: Preheat oven to 425°F (220°C). In a saucepan over medium-high heat, add water, butter and salt. Bring to a boil. Remove from heat and add flour; beat vigorously until mixture forms into a ball. Return to heat for 15 to 20 seconds. Place dough mixture in a food processor fitted with a plastic blade; add 2 eggs. Process until blended. Add remaining 2 eggs; blend again. Scrape sides with a spatula and blend once more.

Lightly grease baking sheets and drop 1" (2.5 cm) mounds of batter onto sheets, shaping as necessary. Bake in upper third of oven 10 to 12 minutes, until puffed, slightly browned and crisp on all sides. Reduce heat to 375°F (190°C) for 10 minutes. Reduce again to 325°F (160°C) for 10 minutes more, then turn oven off for 10 minutes (it's vital that the insides be hollow and dry for splitting).

Filling: In a skillet over medium-high heat, melt butter. Add mushrooms and onion to pan; sauté until tender. Add salt, thyme and flour. Cook, stirring for 1 to 2 minutes, without allowing mixture to brown. Remove from heat. Stir in sour cream.

When ready to serve, cut cream puffs in half. Fill with Mushroom Filling.

MAKES APPROXIMATELY 24

Recipe by George Myketa
Photography: Brian Gould

Pair With:
• Hernder Gewürztraminer
• Soave Bolla

orels Stuffed with Lamb

large fresh morels* (quantity depends on size)
1 lb (500 g) ground lamb
1/4 cup (60 mL) chopped fresh tarragon
1/4 tsp (1 mL) ground cardamom
3 garlic cloves, crushed
1 egg
3 tbsp (45 mL) cracker crumbs

● ● ● ●

Select same-size morels for even cooking. Clean morels and slice lengthwise. Number needed varies between 6 and 20, depending on size. Combine remaining ingredients in a bowl. Stuff each half of morels with lamb mixture. Bake in a glass-baking dish at 350°F (180°C) for 25-35 minutes, until meat mixture is just cooked (no pink colour remains). Smaller morels make a delicious appetizer; larger morels make a great main dish served with salad.

* an edible wild mushroom with a smoky, earthy, nutty flavour

● ● ● ●

SERVES 6

Recipe by George Myketa
Photography: Brian Gould

Pair With:
• Californian Cabernet Sauvignon
• Italian Chianti
• Australian Shiraz

Beef Stuffed with Ricotta & Arugula

3/4 cup (175 mL) fresh ricotta cheese
1/4 cup (60 mL) mascarpone cheese
3 tbsp (45 ml) chopped arugula
1 tsp (5 ml) minced garlic
1 tsp (5 ml) grated lemon zest
24 paper-thin slices bresaola (Italian air-dried, salted beef)
1 bunch arugula for garnish

● ● ● ●

Mix together ricotta, mascarpone, chopped arugula, garlic and lemon zest. Lay 1 bresaola slice on a work surface and put 1 1/2 tbsp (22 mL) of cheese mixture in the centre of the slice. Roll up the slice and place it seam side down on a platter covered with arugula leaves. Repeat with remaining bresaola slices. Cover and refrigerate for 30 minutes before serving.

● ● ● ●

SERVES 8

Recipe by Beatrice Carlani
Photography: Hamid Attie Photography

Pair With:
• Italian Cabernet Sauvignon
• B.C. Cabernet Franc
• Washington State Merlot

Root Vegetable Nests with Poached Quail Eggs & Shaved Black Truffle

2 cups (500 mL) peanut OR canola oil
2 cups (500 mL) assorted potato, sweet potato, parsnip, turnip, beet OR
   any other root vegetable, in a fine julienne
salt
4 quail eggs
1 tsp (15 mL) vinegar
black truffle shavings

● ○ ○ ○

Heat oil in a small saucepan until almost smoking. Oil 2 round soupspoons. Press a mixture of root vegetables between the two spoons. Using the spoons, immerse the root vegetables in hot oil for 45 seconds. Remove spoons and continue to fry nests for another 30 seconds, or until crisp. Remove nests from oil and place on paper towels to drain. Sprinkle with salt. Repeat technique to make 4 nests.

Bring a small saucepan filled with water and a splash of vinegar to a boil; poach quail eggs in water.

Arrange 1 nest in the centre of each of 4 plates; place a quail egg in middle of each nest and top with a black truffle shaving.

● ○ ○ ○

SERVES 4

Recipe by chef Alex Svenne
Photography: Brian Gould

Pair With:
• Orvieto
• Tavel
• B.C. Gamay

Decadent Deviled Eggs with Sturgeon Caviar

8 large hard-boiled eggs, shelled
2 tbsp (30 mL) Dijon mustard
3 tbsp (45 mL) mayonnaise
1 tbsp (15 mL) white wine vinegar
1 tbsp (15 mL) chopped fresh chives
2 oz (60 g) black caviar

● ● ● ●

Slice eggs in half lengthwise; remove yolks. Press yolks through a fine-mesh sieve into a small bowl. Stir in mustard, mayonnaise, vinegar and chives.

Spoon yolk mixture into a pastry bag fitted with a wide tip and fill egg whites.

Garnish with caviar and fresh chive sprigs.

● ● ● ●

MAKES 16

Indonesian Deviled Eggs with Shrimp

6 hard-boiled eggs, shelled
3 tbsp (45 mL) mayonnaise
3/4 tsp (3 mL) Madras curry powder
1/4 tsp (1 mL) ground cinnamon
3 green onions, minced
1/4 cup (60 mL) deveined, shelled, cooked, finely chopped shrimp
salt and pepper, to taste
12 deveined, shelled, cooked shrimp

● ● ● ●

Slice eggs in half lengthwise; remove yolks. In a small bowl, mix yolks, mayonnaise, curry powder, cinnamon, green onions, chopped shrimp; season with salt and pepper. Spoon filling into egg whites. Top each egg with a shrimp.

● ● ● ●

MAKES 12

Recipes by Claudine Gervais
Photography: Brian Gould

rittata Cubes

1 1/2 lbs (750 g) potatoes
1 tbsp (15 mL) olive oil
1 medium onion, chopped
4 garlic cloves, crushed
1 red bell pepper, cored, seeded and chopped
salt and pepper, to taste
10 eggs
1/2 tsp (2 mL) hot pepper sauce

● ● ● ●

In a large pot of salted water over medium-high heat, bring potatoes to a boil and cook until fork tender, approximately 15 minutes. Remove from heat, drain potatoes and allow to cool; cut each potato into thin slices. Coat a 9 x 13" (23 x 33 cm) baking pan with cooking spray; arrange potatoes in pan.

In a skillet over medium heat, heat oil; add onion, garlic and red pepper and sauté until tender. Spoon onion mixture over potato slices and season with salt and pepper. Whisk eggs with hot pepper sauce; pour over vegetables in baking pan. Place in 325°F (160°C) oven and bake until egg mixture has set, approximately 35 to 40 minutes. Allow to cool; cut into 3/4" (2 cm) cubes. Serve as is or skewer cubes individually or thread alternating with grape tomatoes and olives. Try pairing these frittata cubes with your favourite tomato sauce as a dip.

● ● ● ●

MAKES 24 CUBES

Recipe by Claudine Gervais
Photography: Brian Gould

Chicken Liver Pâté

2 lbs (1 kg) chicken livers
1 cup (250 mL) chopped bacon, 1"/2.5 cm pieces
1 small onion, chopped
1 head of garlic, chopped (10-12 cloves)
2 tbsp (30 mL) bread crumbs
2 eggs
1/4 cup (60 mL) whipping cream
1 oz (30 mL) brandy (optional)
1 tsp (5 mL) salt
1 tsp (5 mL) coarse black pepper

● ● ● ●

Purée livers, bacon, onions and garlic in a food processor. Add bread crumbs, eggs, cream, brandy, if using, salt and pepper. Mix well.

Line a loaf pan with foil. Pour in liver mixture. Bake at 300°F (150°C) for 45 minutes, until firm. For a softer pâté, cover with foil. Place loaf pan in water bath, this will add 15 minutes to the cooking time.

Serve with crackers and gherkins.

● ● ● ●

Recipe by chef Alex Svenne
Photography: Brian Gould

Pair With:
• Lakeview Riesling

Goose Liver Foie Gras with Muscat Zabaglione & Lingonberries

Muscat Zabaglione:
4 egg yolks
1/4 cup (60 mL) Muscat wine

1 tbsp (15 mL) canola oil
4, 2 oz (60 g) slices of **goose liver** foie gras, cleaned and trimmed
4 thin slices of white baguette
1/4 cup (60 mL) lingonberry preserves

● ● ● ●

Zabaglione: In a stainless-steel bowl set over a pot of boiling water, whisk egg yolks until foamy. Add wine and whip until doubled in volume and temperature reaches 140°F (60°C).

Brush a skillet with oil. Over medium heat, sear foie gras on 1 side until it reaches a beautiful mahogany colour.

Arrange a slice of foie gras on each slice of baguette. Place in centre of each of 4 plates. Drape with zabaglione and garnish with a spoonful of lingonberry preserves.

● ● ● ●

SERVES 4

Recipe by chef Alex Svenne
Photography: Brian Gould

Pair With:
• Sauternes
• Late Harvest Muscat
• Amontillado Sherry

Duck Confit Terrine with Caramelized Shallots, Port & Figs

Duck Confit:
1 duck (Moulard)
1 tbsp (15 mL) kosher salt
2 bay leaves
1 tsp (5 mL) thyme
1 tsp (5 mL) rosemary
1 tsp (5 mL) peppercorns
1 tsp (5 mL) chopped garlic
1 tbsp (15 mL) brown sugar

Duck Stock:
roasted bones from 1 duck
1 small onion, peeled and
    chopped
1 carrot
3 whole cloves
3 peppercorns
1 bay leaf
1/2 tsp (2 mL) salt

Caramelized Shallots:
1 tbsp (15 mL) butter
2 cups (500 mL) peeled
    shallots
1/2 tsp (2 mL) salt
1/4 cup (60 mL) balsamic
    vinegar

Port-Marinated Figs:
6 dried Calimyrna (Smyrna)
    figs
1/2 cup (125 mL) ruby port

Duck Aspic:
2 cups (500 mL) cold duck
    stock
1 tbsp (15 mL) powdered
    gelatin
1 oz (30 mL) cognac

truffle oil

Duck Confit Terrine with Caramelized Shallots, Port & Figs *(continued)*

● ○ ○ ○

Confit: Remove breasts and legs from duck (save breast meat for another purpose). Trim any extra fat and skin from legs and breasts. Roast duck carcass with any scraps of skin and fat at 300°F (150°C) until bones are golden brown. Drain off rendered fat and reserve. Save bones for stock. Combine salt and seasonings. Coat legs with salt mixture. Place legs in a glass casserole; cover and refrigerate for 2 to 3 days.

Rinse salt from duck legs and blot dry. Place legs in a deep casserole. Melt reserved duck fat and pour over legs, immersing completely. Cover casserole and bake at 300°F (150°C) for 3 hours, or until legs are very tender. Cool duck in its fat and let sit, covered, in the refrigerator for 1 to 2 days to blend the flavours.

Stock: Place duck bones in a stock pot. Cover with cold water. Water should be 2" (5 cm) over bones. On medium heat, bring water to a simmer. Skim any fat that rises to the top. Continue to simmer and skim (this might take 45 minutes). Do not let stock boil! Add onion, carrot and seasonings. Simmer for 3 hours. Strain stock. Strain once more through several layers of cheesecloth. If stock still looks grainy, strain again. Return stock to a clean pot and bring to a low boil. Simmer until reduced by half. Strain stock again through several layers of cheesecloth. Chill.

Shallots: Melt butter and sauté shallots with salt until soft and starting to brown. Add balsamic vinegar and simmer until vinegar is reduced.

Figs: Heat port to a low simmer. Pour over figs. Let sit for 2 to 3 hours or overnight. Most of the port will be absorbed.

Aspic: Skim any remaining fat from duck stock. If cold stock is already a firm gel, you won't need the gelatin. If soft or runny, add gelatin. Heat stock to a low boil; add cognac and simmer. Add salt if needed. Dissolve gelatin in 1/4 cup (60 mL) cold water. Stir into stock and mix until completely dissolved.

To Assemble: Line a loaf pan or terrine mould with plastic wrap. Slice figs, and arrange on bottom of pan. Layer duck meat on top of figs. Layer shallots on top of duck. Repeat until terrine is filled 1" (2.5 cm) from the top. Pour hot aspic over terrine. Tap pan on counter to allow aspic to seep all the way through. Cover with plastic wrap. Place a second loaf pan on top to weigh down terrine. Refrigerate overnight.

Serve on a platter garnished with radicchio and figs. Drizzle with truffle oil.

● ○ ○ ○

Recipe chef Alex Svenne
Photography: Brian Gould

Pair With:
• Gunderloch Nackenheim Roothenber Riesling

Squab Confit with Candied Pecans & Arugula

1/4 cup (60 mL) kosher salt
1 tbsp (15 mL) brown sugar
1 bay leaf, crushed
2 tsp (10 mL) coarsely ground
   black pepper
4 squab OR chicken legs
1 cup + 1 tbsp (265 mL) duck
   fat OR substitute lard if you
   have no other options
1 tbsp (15 mL) butter
1/4 cup (60 mL) pecan pieces
1 tbsp (15 mL) brown sugar
8 oz (250 g) arugula
1 tbsp (15 mL) sherry vinegar

● ● ● ●

In a bowl, combine salt, sugar, bay leaf and pepper. Sprinkle squab with salt mixture; cover, refrigerate and let cure 1 day. Rinse off squab. Preheat oven to 275°F (135°C). In a sauté pan, melt duck fat over medium-low heat. Pour over squab in a small ovenproof pan, immersing completely. Cover and bake for 2 hours. Remove from oven and let cool. For best results, let the legs sit in fat, refrigerated, for a couple of days.

Melt butter in a sauté pan over medium-low heat. Add pecans and sauté; add brown sugar, stirring occasionally, and remove from heat. Let cool.

Remove squab from fat, wiping off any excess. Heat 1 tbsp (15 mL) duck fat in a sauté pan over medium heat. Add squab to pan and fry until skin is crisp. Toss arugula in vinegar and arrange on plates. Lay squash next to arugula and sprinkle plate with pecans.

● ● ● ●

SERVES 4

Recipe by chef Alex Svenne

Photography: Brian Gould

Pair With:
• Oregon Pinot Gris
• California Viognier
• B.C. Chenin Blanc

SOUPS

Chilled Coconut Soup
with Grilled Pineapple & Mango Sorbet

4 cups (1 L) canned unsweetened coconut milk
1 1/2 cups (375 mL) coarsely grated fresh coconut OR unsweetened shredded
1 cup (250 mL) sugar, divided
1 vanilla bean, split lengthwise
1/4 cup (60 mL) fresh lime juice
4-5 lb (1.8-2.2 kg) fresh pineapple, peeled, quartered lengthwise, cored
1 qt (1 L) frozen mango sorbet
mint leaves for garnish
toasted coconut

• • • •

Bring coconut milk, coconut and 1/2 cup (125 mL) sugar to a simmer in a heavy saucepan, whisking until sugar dissolves. Cover and set aside to cool. Strain liquid, pressing on solids to extract flavour. Refrigerate soup until cold. Discard solids.

Preheat a grill to high. Scrape vanilla bean seeds into remaining sugar and mix well. Drizzle lime juice over pineapple quarters and drench in vanilla sugar. Grill pineapple on all sides until a nice caramel colour. Remove from grill and cut into bite-sized pieces. Let stand at room temperature. Ladle soup into 8 funky martini glasses. Top each with a scoop of sorbet and place pineapple around sorbet. Garnish each with a mint leaf and toasted coconut.

• • • •

SERVES 8

Recipe by chef Shelly Martin
Photography: Brian Gould

 Roasted Red Pepper & Tomato Soup with Basil Cream

Roasted Red Pepper & Tomato Soup:
1 tsp (5 mL) olive oil
1 medium onion, finely diced
3 cups (750 mL) peeled, seeded and chopped tomatoes
3 cups (750 mL) chopped roasted red peppers, fresh OR canned
1 cup (250 mL) chicken stock
1/2 cup (125 mL) cream
salt and freshly ground pepper, to taste
1 tsp (5 mL) lemon juice

Basil Cream:
4 tbsp (60 mL) sour cream
2 tbsp (30 mL) whipping cream
1 tbsp (15 mL) fresh basil chiffonade*

● ● ● ●

Soup: In a large skillet, heat oil over medium heat and sauté onion until tender. Add tomatoes and roasted peppers. Cover and cook for 15 minutes. Purée sautéed vegetables in blender. Return purée to saucepan. Add stock and cream. Stir well. Simmer, uncovered, over low heat for 10 minutes. Season to taste with salt and pepper; stir in lemon juice. To serve, top each serving with a spoonful of basil cream.

Cream: Combine all ingredients, mixing well.

* Chiffonade means finely shredded.

● ● ● ●

SERVES 4

Recipe by chef Stephan Joachim
Photography: Brian Gould

Pair With:
• Burdon Amontillado sherry
• Fontanafredda's Barbera D'Alba
• A shot of Grey Goose Vodka served frozen from the freezer.

Charred Tomato Soup with Roasted Garlic & Sour Cream

1 cup (250 mL) sour cream
2 tbsp (30 mL) finely chopped
  green onion
1 tbsp (15 mL) finely chopped
  parsley
freshly cracked black pepper

Tomato Soup:

1 head of garlic, top cut off
  and drizzled with olive oil
  and sea salt
12 large, ripe Roma tomatoes
2 tbsp (30 mL) olive oil
3 cups (750 mL) smoked chicken
  stock OR boxed chicken stock
2 tsp (10 mL) light brown sugar

• • • •

Combine sour cream, green onions, parsley and pepper in a bowl. Cover and chill.

Soup: Preheat oven to 400°F (200°C). Wrap garlic in aluminum foil. Bake for 30 minutes, or until softened. Remove from oven and let cool.

Preheat grill to high. Cut tomatoes in half and brush skin side with olive oil. Place skin side of tomato on grill and cook until charred. Remove from heat. Reduce oven temperature to 350°F (180°C). Place tomatoes on a baking sheet lined with parchment paper and bake for 20 to 30 minutes, or until very soft. Remove from heat and allow to cool slightly.

Squeeze garlic pulp into a blender or food processor. Add tomatoes (in batches if necessary) and process until smooth. Pour tomato mixture into a pot; add chicken stock and sugar, stirring to combine. Simmer for 10 minutes. Ladle into soup bowls; garnish with sour cream mixture and serve immediately.

• • • •

SERVES 4

Recipe by Brandon Boone
Photography: Brian Gould

Pair With:
• Orvieto
• Hungarian Pinot Gris
• Groener Veltliner

Carrot Soup with Blood Orange & Tarragon

1 tbsp (15 mL) butter
3/4 cup (175 mL) chopped onion
1 lb (500 g) peeled carrots, chopped
3 cups (750 mL) vegetable stock
1/2 cup (125 mL) blood orange juice
1 tbsp (15 mL) brandy
2 tsp (10 mL) chopped fresh tarragon
salt and pepper, to taste

1 blood orange, thinly sliced
4 tbsp (60 mL) yogurt, divided
fresh tarragon sprigs

● ● ● ●

Melt butter in large heavy-bottomed saucepan over medium heat. Add onion and carrots; sauté until onion is soft, about 8 minutes. Add stock; cover and bring to a boil. Reduce heat, uncover and simmer until carrots are tender, about 10 minutes.

Working in batches, purée soup in blender until very smooth. Return soup to pot. Stir in orange juice, brandy and chopped tarragon; let simmer 5 minutes. Season with salt and pepper to taste. Divide into 4 bowls and garnish each serving with a couple of blood orange slices, 1 tbsp (15 mL) yogurt and tarragon sprigs. Serve immediately.

● ● ● ●

SERVES 4 TO 5

Recipe by chef Mark Klaudt

Photography: John Ulan/Epic Photography

Pair With:
• B.C. Sauvignon Blanc
• White Bordeaux
• California White Zinfandel

Curried Carrot Soup

1/4 cup (60 mL) olive oil
1 1/2 tsp (7 mL) curry powder
1 tsp (5 mL) garam masala
8 medium-sized carrots, shredded
4 celery stalks, coarsely chopped
4 green onions, coarsely chopped
1 yellow onion, coarsely chopped
5 cups (1.25 L) chicken stock
1/2 tsp (2 mL) coarsely ground black pepper
fresh lemon wedges

• • • •

Heat oil in a large heavy-bottomed saucepan over medium heat; add curry powder and garam masala; cook for 2 minutes, stirring often. Add carrots, celery and onions to pan; sauté to coat with oil. Continue to cook for 10 minutes, stirring often. Add stock to pan and bring to a boil. Lower heat and let simmer for 10 minutes or until vegetables are tender. Allow the soup to sit to let any excess oil rise to the top; skim off oil.

In batches, purée soup in a blender until smooth. Return soup to a clean pan and heat over medium-low heat until hot. Serve immediately.

• • • •

SERVES 4 TO 5

Recipe by chef K.R. Johnson
Photography: Brian Gould

Pair With:
• Alsatian Gewürztraminer
• B.C. Riesling
• India Pale Ale

Butternut Squash & Apple Bisque

1 butternut squash, unpeeled, cut in half, seeded
2 Granny Smith apples, peeled, cored and coarsely chopped
1 yellow onion, coarsely chopped
1/2 tsp (2 mL) dried rosemary
1/4 tsp (1 mL) dried marjoram
4 cups (1 L) chicken stock
2 slices white bread, trimmed and cubed
1/2 tsp (2 mL) salt
1/2 tsp (2 mL) black pepper
2 large egg yolks
1/2 cup (125 mL) whipping cream

● ● ● ●

In a large heavy-bottomed saucepan, combine all ingredients except yolks and cream. Bring to a boil and simmer, uncovered, for 45 minutes, or until vegetables are tender. Remove from heat. Remove the squash halves from the saucepan; let cool and spoon the flesh back into the saucepan.

In batches, purée soup in a blender until smooth. Return soup to a clean pot. In a separate bowl, combine yolks and cream. Whisk 1/2 cup (125 mL) of the puréed soup into the yolk mixture and then stir into the pot of soup. Heat soup over medium-low heat until hot. Serve immediately.

● ● ● ●

SERVES 4

Recipe by chef K.R. Johnson
Photography: Brian Gould

Pair With:
• Amontillado Sherry
• Vintage Sake
• Australian Semillon

Pumpkin Soup with Pancetta & Gorgonzola

2 small pumpkins (try to get sugar pumpkins as opposed to large jack-o'-lantern types) OR or other fleshy squash, such as butternut
1/4 cup (60 mL) olive oil
4 cups (1 L) chicken OR vegetable stock
1 thyme sprig
1 bay leaf
3 whole cloves
8 oz (250 g) pancetta, sliced then finely chopped
1 medium onion, diced
salt and pepper, to taste
4 oz (125 g) Gorgonzola, coarsely crumbled

• • • •

Preheat oven to 350°F (180°C).

Cut pumpkins in half and remove seeds. Oil cut sides and place face down on cookie sheets. Bake for about 45 minutes, until pumpkin is very soft.

Scoop pumpkin meat into soup pot. Add stock, thyme, bay leaf and cloves and bring to a low boil. Simmer for 30 minutes.

Purée soup with a hand blender.

In a skillet over medium-high heat, sauté pancetta and onions until onions are golden and pancetta is crisp. Drain off fat; add pancetta and onions to puréed soup. Check seasoning and add salt and pepper as necessary. Serve soup with crumbled Gorgonzola floating in the middle.

• • • •

SERVES 4

Recipe by chef Alex Svenne
Photography: Brian Gould

Pair With:
• Italian Valpolicella
• Hoegaarden
• B.C. Gamay Noir

Asparagus & Spinach Soup with Asiago Curls

1 1/4 cups (300 mL) finely chopped leeks, white and pale green parts only
2 tbsp (30 mL) unsalted butter
1/2 cup (125 mL) finely chopped shallots
1/4 tsp (1 mL) black pepper
3/4 tsp (4 mL) salt, divided
1/2 tsp (2 mL) nutmeg
2 1/2 lbs (1.25 kg) asparagus, trimmed and cut into 1 1/2" (4 cm) pieces
3 1/2 cups (825 mL) chicken OR vegetable stock
1 1/2 cups (375 mL) water
1 lb (500 g) spinach leaves
1/4 cup (60 mL) whipping cream
Asiago OR Parmesan curls shaved from a wedge with a vegetable peeler
homemade croûtons

• • • •

Wash chopped leeks in a bowl of cold water; then lift out and drain well. Melt butter in a heavy-bottomed skillet over medium-low heat and cook leeks, shallots, pepper, 1/2 tsp (2 mL) salt and nutmeg; continue to cook until leeks are softened, about 3 minutes. Add asparagus, broth and water; simmer, covered, until asparagus is tender, 10 to 12 minutes. After 3 to 4 minutes, remove 6 asparagus tips, halve lengthwise and reserve for garnish. Add spinach to skillet. Working in batches, purée soup in a blender until very smooth.

Pour soup through a sieve into a clean pot. Stir in cream, remaining salt and season with additional pepper to taste. Heat soup over moderately low heat until hot.

• • • •

SERVES 6

Recipe by chef Mark Klaudt
Photography: John Ulan/Epic Photography

Pair With:
• French Viognier
• B.C. Chenin Blanc
• Oregon Pinot Gris

Spinach & Cheese Tortellini Soup

1 tbsp (15 mL) canola oil
1 small onion, chopped
1 garlic clove, minced
1/4 tsp (1 mL) nutmeg
8 cups (2 L) chicken OR vegetable stock
1/2 cup (125 mL) Arborio rice
2 lbs (1 kg) fresh spinach or 10 oz (300 g) pkg frozen
juice and grated zest of 1 lemon
salt and pepper, to taste
1/2 cup (125 mL) sour cream
1 lb (500 g) ricotta tortellini, cooked
fresh spinach chiffonade for garnish

● ● ● ●

Heat oil in a skillet over medium-high heat; add onion and sauté until just starting to brown. Add garlic and sauté for 1 minute. Add nutmeg, stock and rice. Bring to a boil. Simmer until rice is soft. Add spinach, cooking just until fresh spinach is wilted. Add lemon juice and zest. Using a hand blender, purée soup until smooth. Add salt and pepper to taste. Before serving, stir in sour cream. Place tortellini in bowls and fill with hot soup. Garnish with a chiffonade of fresh spinach leaves.

● ● ● ●

SERVES 4

Recipe by chef Alex Svenne
Photography: Brian Gould

Pair With:
• Italian Arneis
• Ontario Chardonnay
• Australian Viognier

eek & Rice Soup

This can be served as a side dish or soup, depending on the amount of water added.

3 tbsp (45 mL) extra-virgin olive oil
1 medium white onion, julienned
6 whole leeks
2 tbsp (30 mL) sea salt, or to taste
1 tsp (5 mL) freshly ground pepper
2 tsp (10 mL) freshly ground nutmeg
4 cups (1 L) diced tomatoes
5 cups (1.25 L) water (for a side dish) OR 10 cups (2.5 L) water (for soup)
3 oz (90 g) tomato paste
1 cup (250 mL) parboiled rice

● ● ● ●

Heat oil in a large saucepan over medium-high heat and sauté onion until soft. Add remaining ingredients, except rice; bring soup to a boil. Add rice; reduce heat to medium and simmer, stirring occasionally, until rice is soft.

● ● ● ●

SERVES 4 TO 5

Recipe by chef Nicky Makris
Photography: Brian Gould

Pair With:
• Italian Pinot Grigio
• Austrian Gruener Veltliner
• B.C. Pinot Auxerrois

Pasta e Fagioli

1 lb (500 g) dry Roma beans
salt and pepper, to taste
1/4 cup (60 mL) olive oil
1 garlic clove, chopped
1 small onion, diced
2 ripe Roma tomatoes, chopped
1 tbsp (15 mL) chopped parsley
7 oz (200 g) tubetti pasta
1/4 cup (60 mL) Parmesan cheese

• • • •

Soak beans overnight in lukewarm water. Next day, rinse beans and place in a large pot. Add enough cold water to cover beans by about 1" (2.5 cm). Add salt and pepper to taste. Cook at low heat, covered, for 1 hour. Check occasionally to make sure that beans do not stick to the bottom of the pot. Add a little more water if required. When beans are cooked, heat oil in a skillet; add garlic and onion and sauté. Add tomatoes and parsley. Cook for 3 minutes and add to beans.

In a separate pot, filled with boiling salted water, cook pasta al dente (slightly undercooked). Drain and add to beans. Allow all ingredients to cook together for another 2 minutes and turn off heat. Let soup rest for a few minutes before ladling into deep plates. Sprinkle with Parmesan cheese and serve.

• • • •

SERVES 4

Recipe by Anna Dell'Acqua
Photography: Brian Gould

Pair With:
• Italian Orvieto
• B.C. Sauvignon Blanc
• South African Chenin Blanc

Nicky's Lentil Soup

Go for the gusto, Nicky's Lentil Soup has been featured on the Food Network – it's feisty, flavourful and supremely simple to make – over 2 million bowls served!

3 tbsp (45 mL) olive oil
1 medium onion, chopped
4 garlic cloves, chopped
1 carrot, chopped
2 celery stalks, chopped
2 cups (500 mL) diced tomatoes
2 cups (500 mL) tomato juice
3 bay leaves
1 tbsp (15 mL) sea salt, or to taste
1 tbsp (15 mL) fresh dill
2 sprigs Italian parsley, chopped
2 cups (500 mL) lentils
9 cups (2.25 L) chicken stock
6 tbsp (90 mL) tomato paste
1 1/2 tsp (7 mL) pepper

• • • •

Heat oil in a large soup pot over medium heat; add onion, garlic, carrot and celery and sauté until vegetables are almost tender. Add remaining ingredients and bring to a boil, stirring occasionally. Simmer for 1 hour, or until lentils are soft but not breaking apart. Ladle into bowls.

• • • •

SERVES 4 TO 6

Recipe by chef Nicky Makris
Photography: Patricia Holdsworth

Pair With:
• Soave
• India Pale Ale
• Australian Viognier

eatless Borsch

3 beets, size of an orange, cut into thin strips
1 carrot, diced
8 cups (2 L) water
1 medium potato, diced
2 tbsp (30 mL) lemon juice
1/2 cup (125 mL) string beans, green peas OR white beans
1 large onion, sliced
3 tbsp (45 mL) butter
1 1/2 cups (375 mL) shredded cabbage
1 cup (250 mL) tomato juice
1 1/2 tbsp (22 mL) flour
1/2 cup (125 mL) cold water
2 tbsp (30 mL) chopped dillweed
1/2 tsp (2 mL) EACH, salt and pepper
sour cream and chopped dill for garnish (optional)

● ● ● ●

In a large heavy-bottomed saucepan, cook beets and carrots in water for 20 minutes. Add potatoes, simmer 10 to 15 minutes. Add lemon juice (keeps red colour in beets). Add beans or peas. Simmer until tender.

Sauté onion in butter until soft. Add cabbage to onions with 1/4 cup (60 mL) water, simmer until cabbage is tender. Stir into beets. Add tomato juice. Blend flour with 1/2 cup (125 mL) cold water, stir into vegetables. Add dill for added flavour. Bring to a boil. Stir in salt and pepper. Serve hot with a dollop of sour cream and a sprinkle of chopped dill, if you wish.

● ● ● ●

SERVES 15

Recipe courtesy of *Ukrainian Daughters' Cookbook*
Photography: Patricia Holdsworth

Sunset Corn Chowder

The Base:

2 cups (500 mL) fresh OR frozen corn
1 cup (250 mL) EACH, diced white onion,
   carrot and celery
4 garlic cloves, peeled and chopped
4 cups (1 L) chicken stock
1/2 cup (125 mL) cooked brown rice
2 tbsp (30 mL) ground cumin
1 tsp (5 mL) ground turmeric
1 tbsp (15 mL) chopped chipotle peppers,
   dried or canned
1 tbsp (15 mL) salt, or more to taste

Additions:

1/2 cup (125 mL) whipping cream
1 cup (250 mL) fresh or frozen corn
1/2 cup (125 mL) EACH, red and green
   pepper, small dice
1/2 cup (125 mL) zucchini, small dice
1/2 cup (125 mL) cooked black beans

Final Touch:

1/2 lb (250 g) cooked chicken, shredded
2 tbsp (30 mL) EACH, chopped fresh
   oregano and cilantro
1 lime, cut into wedges
corn tortilla chips

● ● ● ●

Base: Place all ingredients in a large heavy saucepan and bring to a boil. Reduce heat and simmer for 20 minutes, or until all vegetables are soft. Using a blender or a food processor, purée mixture as finely as possible. Strain through a fine mesh strainer, pressing down on solids to extract as much liquid as possible, then return to pot and return to simmer.

Additions: Add all ingredients to base and simmer for an additional 10 to 15 minutes, or until all vegetables are tender but firm. Adjust seasoning with more chipotle peppers or your favourite hot sauce.

Ladle equal portions of soup into bowls and top with chicken and herbs. Accompany with lime wedges and corn tortilla chips. Serve immediately.

● ● ● ●

SERVES 4

Recipe by chef Stephan MacIntyre
Photography: Hamid Attie Photography

Pair With:

• Italian Arneis
• B.C. Pinot Gris
• Australian Semillon

Hot & Sour Soup with Smoked Chicken Stock

4 cups (1 L) smoked chicken stock, page 92 OR boxed chicken stock
2 stalks lemon grass, white ends only, cut in half
1/2" (1/3 cm) piece of ginger, thinly sliced
3 kaffir lime leaves*
1 boneless, skinless chicken breast, cut into 1/4" (6 mm) dice
3 tbsp (45 mL) fish sauce
1/4 cup (60 mL) lime juice
2 red chiles, seeded and thinly sliced
8 large shrimp
10 snow peas, julienned
1/2 cup (125 mL) bean sprouts
1 carrot, julienned
2 green onions, thinly sliced on the diagonal
1 red bell pepper, seeded, thinly sliced
fresh cilantro

• • • •

Combine chicken stock, lemon grass, ginger and lime leaves in a large pot; bring to a boil. Reduce heat to simmer, cover, and let cook 20 minutes. Remove lemon grass, ginger and lime leaves. Bring stock back to a boil. Add chicken, fish sauce, lime juice and chiles to pot. Simmer for 5 minutes. Add shrimp and cook for an additional 2 minutes.

Divide snow peas, bean sprouts, carrot, green onions and red pepper evenly between 2 bowls. Ladle soup into bowls and serve immediately.

*Kaffir lime leaves are available in Asian food stores and some large supermarkets.

• • • •

SERVES 2

Recipe by Brandon Boone
Photography: Brian Gould

Pair With:
• Green Tea
• Indian Pale Ale
• Mexican Lager

Smoked Wild Turkey Consommé with Sage Dumplings

1 smoked wild turkey carcass OR 3 lbs (1.5 kg) assorted smoked skin-on turkey parts (such as necks, legs and wing tips)
2 large onions, chopped
2 celery stalks, chopped
1 large carrot, chopped
2 tsp (10 mL) peppercorns
2 dried bay leaves
1 tsp (5 mL) salt
1/2 cup (125 mL) cognac
1 cup (250 mL) flour
1 egg
1/4 cup (60 mL) water
1 tbsp (15 mL) chopped fresh sage

• • • •

Place turkey carcass (or smoked turkey parts) in a large stockpot and cover with water; bring to a gentle simmer. Regularly skim fat that floats to the top. When very little fat remains, add vegetables and seasonings. Simmer for 4 hours. Strain stock and refrigerate overnight. The next day skim fat on surface.

In a large stockpot over medium-high heat, boil cognac until almost evaporated. Add turkey stock and bring to a simmer. Continue to cook until reduced by half; season with salt and pepper.

In a mixing bowl, combine flour, egg, water and sage to make a soft sticky dough. Drop teaspoonfuls of dough into simmering stock and simmer for 10 to 15 minutes. Remove dumplings from consommé as cooked. Serve a few dumplings in each bowl with consommé.

• • • •

SERVES 4

Recipe by chef Alex Svenne
Photography: Brian Gould

Pair With:
• Rioja Rosé
• Nut Brown Ale
• White Bordeaux

B rodo di Pollo (Wedding Soup)

1 chicken carcass, most of meat removed
2 celery stalks, chopped
1/2 medium onion, chopped
4-5 seeded fresh tomatoes, chopped (seeds can impart a bitter taste)
salt and pepper, to taste

Meatballs:
2/3 lb (350 g) ground veal
1 tsp (5 mL) salt
1/2 tsp (2 mL) pepper
4 oz (125 g) freshly grated Parmesan cheese
4 slices stale bread, crushed into crumbs
handful of chopped parsley, leaves only
2 eggs, beaten
olive oil

1 pkg pasta, such as baby pasta shells
Parmesan cheese for garnish

• • • •

Combine chicken carcass, celery, onion, tomatoes, salt and pepper in a large Dutch oven. Cover with water. Bring to a boil; simmer several hours. Strain, reserving liquid.

Meatballs: In a bowl, combine all ingredients, except oil. If mixture is too dry, add another egg; if too wet, add more cheese and breadcrumbs. Refrigerate for several hours, if possible. With hands moistened and coated with a small amount of olive oil, form meat mixture into very tiny meatballs, slightly larger than chickpeas. Fry quickly in olive oil. Do not cook through. Drain on paper towels. (Frying meatballs before adding to soup keeps it from turning cloudy when they are added to broth.) Bring broth to a boil. Reduce to a simmer; add meatballs. Simmer for 45 minutes.

In a separate pot, cook pasta to halfway point. Add partially cooked pasta to soup and cook until al dente. Ladle soup into bowls and garnish with Parmesan.

• • • •

Recipe by Gina Giambattista

Photography: Patricia Holdsworth

Pair With:
• Italian Trebbiano
• B.C. White Meritage
• Spanish White Rioja

Clam, Italian Sausage & Tomato Soup

Italian soups are usually highly flavoured with lots of garlic, onions and hearty herbs such as sage, rosemary or oregano.

1 tbsp (15 mL) olive oil
1 onion, diced
1 garlic clove, minced
pinch of chile flakes
1 EACH, red and green bell pepper, diced
1 tsp (5 mL) dried oregano
1/2 tsp (2 mL) dried thyme
2 hot Italian sausages, cooked and cut into 1/2" (1.3 cm) pieces
28 oz (796 mL) can diced tomatoes with juice
2 tbsp (30 mL) tomato paste
4 cups (1 L) water OR stock
1 lb (500 g) live clams, cleaned
grated lemon zest for garnish

• • • •

Heat oil in a skillet over medium-high heat; add onion and sauté until just starting to brown. Add garlic and chiles, sauté 1 minute. Add peppers, herbs and sausage. Sauté for 3 to 5 minutes. Add tomatoes, tomato paste and water. Bring to a boil, cover and reduce heat to a simmer. About 20 minutes before serving, bring soup back to a boil, add clams and steam until clams open, discarding any that don't. Garnish with lemon zest.

• • • •

SERVES 4

Recipe by chef Alex Svenne
Photography: Brian Gould

Pair With:
• Italian Pinot Grigio
• German Troken Riesling
• French Burgundy Aligoté

(P)ozole with Pitillal Chile Sauce

Pozole:
2 lbs (1 kg) pork side ribs OR bone-in roast, cut into large pieces
1 large white onion, halved and thinly sliced
1 head of garlic, chopped
8 cups (2 L) cold water
4 cups (1 L) chicken stock
2, 29 oz (796 mL) cans white hominy corn, drained and rinsed
salt and pepper to taste

Pitillal Chile Sauce:
10 dried red chiles
1/2 cup (125 mL) water
2 garlic cloves
1/3 cup (75 mL) canola oil
additional water, as needed

Accompaniments:
2 cups (500 mL) shredded lettuce OR cabbage
1 cup (250 mL) sliced radishes
10 key limes, halved
1/2 cup (125 mL) dried oregano
1/2 cup (125 mL) diced white onion

• • • •

Pozole: Place pork in a large stockpot with onion and garlic; add cold water. Bring to a boil, reduce heat and simmer for 2 hours, or until meat is falling off the bone. Add chicken stock and corn; season with salt and pepper to taste. Simmer for 1 hour.

Sauce: Add chiles to a medium-sized skillet over medium heat and sauté for 2 minutes; cover with 1/2 cup (125 mL) water. Cook for 3 to 5 minutes, or until chiles begin to soften. Pour chiles and water into a blender; pulse to make a thick paste. Add more water if necessary. Add garlic and continue to blend. Return paste to the skillet and cook over medium-low heat until almost dry. Remove from heat and add canola oil. Mix into a paste. Caution: this sauce is extremely hot. Avoid contact with eyes or broken skin.

Ladle soup into large bowls, top with a small amount of Pitillal Chile sauce and add accompaniments as desired.

• • • •

SERVES 12

Recipe by Miriam Zolkewich
Photography: Brian Gould

Kentucky Burgoo Soup

The Night Before:
1 lb (500 g) stewing beef, in 1" (2.5 cm) pieces
1 lb (500 g) lamb shoulder, in 1" (2.5 cm) pieces
1 lb (500 g) chicken thighs, boneless, skinless, in 1" (2.5 cm) pieces
1 small smoked pork hock (1/2 lb/250 g) OR smoked ham end
4 cups (1 L) good-quality beef stock
19 oz (540 mL) can diced tomatoes
10 oz (284 mL) can tomato paste
2 cups (500 mL) medium-diced white onion
4 garlic cloves, peeled and sliced
1/2 cup (125 mL) Worcestershire sauce
1/4 cup (60 mL) molasses
1/4 cup (60 mL) brown sugar
3 tbsp (45 mL) red wine vinegar
1 tbsp (15 mL) chili powder
1 tbsp (15 mL) hot sauce, or more!

The Next Morning:
2 cups (500 mL) medium diced celery
2 cups (500 mL) medium diced green cabbage
2 cups (500 mL) medium diced carrots
2 cups (500 mL) medium diced potatoes

One Hour to Go:
2 cups (500 mL) fresh or frozen corn
2 cups (500 mL) sliced fresh or frozen okra
1/2 cup (125 mL) chopped parsley
1 tbsp (15 mL) salt, or more to taste
1 tbsp (15 mL) freshly ground black pepper

• • • •

Night Before: Preheat oven to 200°F (100°C). Place all ingredients in a roaster or large pot, stir well and cover; place in the centre of the oven to cook overnight.

Next Morning: Skim any fat from the simmering stew. Mix in all vegetables, cover and return to oven for 6 to 7 hours.

One Hour to Go: Remove pork hock; pull and shred meat and return to pot. Add corn, okra and parsley. Season to taste with salt and pepper then return to oven to heat through. Bring entire pot to table and ladle stew into large bowls.

• • • •

SERVES 8

Recipe by chef Stephan MacIntyre
Photography: Hamid Attie Photography

Pair With:
• Chianti Classico
• California White Meritage
• Washington State Merlot

moked Chicken Stock

Using hickory chips to smoke the chicken bones before making the stock adds a unique and delicious flavour to the end result.

3 lbs (1.5 kg) smoked chicken bones (backs and necks are best)
2 tbsp (30 mL) olive oil
2 onions, diced
2 carrots with green ends attached, washed and diced
2 celery stalks, chopped
2 garlic cloves
8 qts (8 L) cold water
10 Tellicherry peppercorns
1 bunch of parsley, washed and tied tightly together with butcher's string
3 bay leaves
kosher salt

• • • •

If using a charcoal or propane grill for smoking, set up grill for indirect cooking. Soak 2 cups (500 mL) hickory chips in water for 2 hours. Remove from water. Place chips in the centre of 2 layers of heavy-duty aluminum foil. Fold up to form a pouch, folding over edges to seal. Pierce top several times to allow smoke to escape. Once the grill is preheated, place chips on the hot side. Once smoke begins to release, place chicken bones on the cool side. Smoke bones for about 1 hour, or until wood chips stop smoking.

Preheat oven to 400°F (200°C). Place smoked chicken bones in a heavy-duty roaster and drizzle with olive oil. Add onions, carrots, celery and garlic.

Place in oven and roast approximately 1 hour, or until bones reach a deep brown. Transfer all ingredients from roaster into a large stockpot. Add water, peppercorns, parsley and bay leaves. Bring to a boil, uncovered, then reduce heat to a simmer. Continue to cook for 3 hours. Strain stock through a fine sieve lined with cheesecloth. Repeat. Season stock generously with salt. Allow to cool, then place stock in refrigerator for a minimum of 12 hours.

Remove all solidified fat from the surface and portion into freezable containers. Refrigerated stock should last approximately 3 days.

• • •

MAKES 3 1/2 QUARTS (3.5 L)

Recipe by Brandon Boone
Photography: Brian Gould

SALADS

Dressings,
Condiments,
Sauces,
Chutneys, Rubs
Vegetables
& Side Dishes

Field Greens with Roast Cherry, Hazelnut Oil & Balsamic Vinegar Reduction

1/2 cup (125 mL) balsamic vinegar
1 cup (250 mL) sour cherries
1 tbsp (15 mL) canola oil
1/2 cup (125 mL) hazelnuts
8 oz (250 g) mixed field greens
1/4 cup (60 mL) hazelnut oil*
freshly ground pepper

• • • •

In a saucepan over medium-high heat, bring balsamic vinegar to a boil; remove from heat and add cherries to pot. Let cherries soak for a couple of hours or overnight.

Preheat oven to 300°F (150°C). Drain cherries, reserving balsamic vinegar. Pat cherries dry; toss with canola oil to coat. Spread cherries on a cookie sheet and roast for 30 minutes (they should be just starting to shrivel).

In a small saucepan set over medium-high heat, bring reserved balsamic vinegar to a boil; continue to cook until reduced to 2 tbsp (30 mL).

Spread hazelnuts on a baking sheet and toast in oven for 10 minutes.

Divide mixed greens between 2 plates. Sprinkle with toasted hazelnuts and roasted cherries. Drizzle greens with balsamic reduction and hazelnut oil. Sprinkle with freshly ground pepper.

* Nut oils are available at specialty food stores and large supermarkets.

• • • •

SERVES 2

Recipe by chef Alex Svenne
Photography: Brian Gould

Pear, Yellow Tomato & Spinach Salad with Honey, Balsamic Vinegar & Dijon Dressing

Honey, Balsamic Vinegar & Dijon Dressing:
3 tbsp (45 mL) extra-virgin olive oil
1 1/2 tbsp (22 mL) balsamic vinegar
1 tsp (5 mL) honey
1/2 tsp (2 mL) Dijon mustard
1 garlic clove, minced
1/2 tsp (2 mL) dried oregano
salt and pepper to taste

5 oz (180 g) baby spinach leaves, washed and trimmed
1 hard-boiled egg
pinch of paprika
1 Anjou pear, thinly sliced
1 yellow tomato, quartered
1 purple onion, thinly sliced
salt and pepper to taste

• • • •

Dressing: Combine all ingredients, except salt and pepper, in a small bowl. Whisk together and season with salt and pepper to taste.

Place a handful of spinach leaves on each of 2 plates. Remove yolk from hard-boiled egg; dice egg white and place in a single line on top of spinach; crumble yolk on top of the white; sprinkle paprika on top of egg. Arrange pear slices, tomato wedges and onion on spinach. Drizzle dressing over salad and season with salt and pepper.

• • • •

SERVES 2

Recipe by Colin Gandier
Photography: Brian Gould

B istro Salad with Fennel, Pears & Walnuts in a Roquefort White Beer Dressing

Roquefort White Beer Dressing:

4 oz (125 g) Roquefort cheese
1/2 cup (125 mL) mayonnaise
1/2 cup (125 mL) Belgian white beer
1/2 cup (125 mL) 14% sour cream
1/4 cup (60 mL) chives
1 tbsp (15 mL) fresh lemon juice
1 tbsp (15 mL) Worcestershire sauce
1 tsp (5 mL) Tabasco sauce

2 bunches arugula
1 head Boston leaf lettuce
1 head frisée
1 1/2 cups (375 mL) Roquefort dressing (above)
1 fennel bulb, thinly sliced
2 pears, sliced into thin wedges
1/2 cup (125 mL) candied walnuts
2 tbsp (30 mL) chopped fresh chervil

• • • •

Dressing: Whip cheese and mayonnaise together until smooth or leave it a little chunky if that is your preference. Stir in remaining ingredients and mix thoroughly. Refrigerate and allow to thicken for at least 8 hours. Yield: 2 1/2 cups (625 mL)

Place greens in a bowl and toss with salad dressing. Arrange greens on individual plates.

Scatter fennel, pears and walnuts randomly over lettuce and garnish with chervil. Serve immediately.

• • • •

SERVES 8

Recipe by chef Brian Morin
Photography: Brian Gould

Pair With:
• A German-style wheat beer such as Hacker-Pschorr Weisse or Spinnakers Hefeweizen

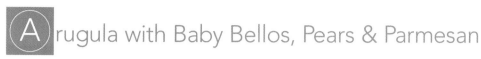rugula with Baby Bellos, Pears & Parmesan

When portobello mushrooms are harvested young, while still in the "button" shape, they are called baby bellos or cremini.

Honey & Shallot Dressing:
2 tbsp (30 mL) red wine vinegar
1 tbsp (15 mL) honey
1 tbsp (15 mL) finely minced shallot
1/3 cup (75 mL) olive oil
salt and pepper

Mushrooms:
1 tbsp (15 mL) butter
1 tbsp (15 mL) olive oil
8 oz (250 g) baby bello mushrooms, finely sliced
1 tbsp (15 mL) finely minced shallot
2 garlic cloves, finely minced
1/4 cup (60 mL) dry white wine

Salad:
6 oz (175 g) arugula
1 semi-ripe pear
4 oz (120 g) piece of Parmesan cheese

• • • •

Dressing: Combine vinegar, honey and shallot in a bowl; slowly add oil in a steady stream, whisking continuously. Season with salt and pepper to taste.

Mushrooms: Heat butter and oil in a skillet over medium-high heat. Add mushrooms, shallot and garlic to pan; sauté until mushrooms begin to brown. Deglaze with white wine and remove from heat. Let cool to room temperature.

Toss arugula with dressing and divide among 4 plates. Cut pear in half and core, using a melon baller. Slice both halves into thin slices and divide among 4 plates; top with warm mushrooms. Using a vegetable peeler, cut 8 Parmesan curls and place 2 on each plate. Serve immediately.

• • • •

SERVES 4

Recipe by Brandon Boone
Photography: Brian Gould

Pair With:
• California Chardonnay
• Côtes du Rhône White
• Ontario Chardonnay

Baby Spinach with Red Onion, Fennel, Pancetta & Parmesan Crisps

1/2 lb (250 g) spicy Italian pancetta, sliced
1/2 cup (125 mL) grated Parmesan cheese

Pancetta Dijon Vinaigrette:

1 egg yolk
1 tbsp (15 mL) Dijon mustard
1 garlic clove, minced
1/4 cup (60 mL) warm drippings from pancetta
1/4 cup (60 mL) white wine vinegar OR tarragon vinegar
1/4 cup (60 mL) olive oil
salt and pepper, to taste

16 oz (500 g) baby spinach
1 small red onion, julienned
1 fennel bulb, julienned

● ● ● ●

In a skillet over medium heat, sauté pancetta until crisp. Remove from pan and reserve drippings. Chop pancetta into bite-size pieces.

Preheat oven to 350°F (180°C). Sprinkle Parmesan on a cookie sheet lined with parchment paper and bake for 10 to 15 minutes, or until cheese bubbles. Remove from oven and cool; cut baked Parmesan into triangles.

Vinaigrette: In a small bowl, whisk egg yolk with mustard and garlic; drizzle in pancetta drippings, oil and vinegar, whisking constantly. Season with salt and pepper to taste.

Toss spinach, onion, fennel and pancetta with vinaigrette. Garnish with Parmesan triangles.

● ● ● ●

SERVES 4

Recipe by chef Alex Svenne
Photography: Brian Gould

Pair With:
● Pale Ale
● New Zealand Sauvignon Blanc
● Beaujolais Villages

Butterleaf, Radish & Honey Ham Salad

The effervescence of the champagne in the dressing really makes this recipe pop. Instead of buying a big bottle, pick a smaller (piccolo) bottle since champagne won't last long once uncorked.

Champagne, Shallot & Dijon Dressing:
3 tbsp (45 mL) olive oil
1 tbsp (15 mL) champagne
1 tbsp (15 mL) garlic-infused white wine vinegar
1 shallot, finely minced
2 tsp (10 mL) Dijon mustard
1 tsp (15 mL) minced parsley
salt and pepper, to taste

2 heads butterleaf lettuce
2 carrots, julienned
3 thinly sliced radishes
4 oz (120 g) honey ham, diced

• • • •

Dressing: Combine oil, champagne, vinegar, shallot, mustard and parsley; whisk to blend. Season with salt and pepper.

Divide lettuce among 4 plates. Drizzle with dressing and top with carrots, radishes and ham. Serve immediately.

• • • •

SERVES 4

Recipe by Brandon Boone
Photography: Brian Gould

Pair With:
• B.C. Pinot Blanc
• Soave
• Côtes du Rhône Rosé

Bocconcini Wrapped in Prosciutto & Grilled Radicchio

This is more method than recipe, having no exact measurements except for the vinaigrette. Make as many or as few as you want.

Sour Cherry Vinaigrette:
3 cups (750 mL) sour cherry syrup
3 cups (750 mL) red wine vinegar
1/4 cup (60 mL) shallots, finely diced
1 tsp (5 mL) EACH, salt and black pepper

Per serving:
bocconcini
salt and black pepper
dried oregano
prosciutto, thinly sliced
radicchio
olive oil
field greens
sun-dried cherries
Parmesan cheese

• • • •

Vinaigrette: Whisk all ingredients together.

Cut bocconcini in half, season with salt, pepper and oregano. Wrap with a piece of prosciutto. Wrap with a radicchio leaf. Drizzle with oil, season with salt and pepper and grill over high heat until cheese softens.

Arrange field greens in the middle of a plate. Coat grilled radicchio with a little vinaigrette and arrange around greens (2 pieces for lunch, 3 for dinner). Pour more vinaigrette onto plate and garnish with sun-dried cherries and shaved Parmesan.

• • • •

Recipe by chef Kevin Lendrum
Photography: John Ulan/Epic Photography

Pair With:
• Italian Primitivo di Manduria
• California Zinfandel
• Oregon Pinot Noir

Baked Camembert on Field Greens with Fig Vinaigrette

4 oz (120 g) Camembert
1/4 cup (60 mL) olive oil
1 tsp (5 mL) balsamic vinegar
salt and freshly cracked black pepper
2 tbsp (30 mL) fresh orange juice
1 tbsp (15 mL) fresh lime juice
2 dried figs, stemmed and diced
4 cups (1 L) mixed field greens

• • • •

Cut cheese into 4 equal portions. In a small bowl combine oil and vinegar. Dip each piece of cheese into mixture making sure to touch vinegar at the bottom. Place cheese on a heatproof plate with plenty of space between pieces and dust with freshly cracked black pepper. Cover and refrigerate. In the same bowl, combine juices and figs. Cover and refrigerate overnight.

Season fig vinaigrette with salt and pepper to taste. Toss field greens with vinaigrette and divide among 4 plates. Preheat oven to 425°F (220°C). Uncover cheese and bake in oven for 10 minutes, or until cheese begins to melt without completely losing its shape. Remove cheese from oven and place 1 piece on salad on each plate. Top with remaining vinaigrette and serve immediately.

• • • •

SERVES 4

Recipe by Brandon Boone
Photography: Brian Gould

Pair With:
• B.C. Gamay Noir
• Valpolicella
• Beaujolais

Goat Cheese Salad
with Maple Eggplant Chutney

Maple Eggplant Chutney:
2 small eggplants cut into 1/4" (6 mm) slices
1 tsp (5 mL) salt
2 tbsp (30 mL) extra-virgin olive oil
2 red onions, finely chopped
2 garlic cloves, finely minced
1/4 cup (60 mL) maple syrup
2 tbsp (15 mL) red currant jelly
1/2 cup (125 mL) dry white wine
1 tbsp (15 mL) aged balsamic vinegar
1/4 cup (60 mL) chopped chives
salt and pepper to taste

mixed baby salad greens, as needed
8 oz (250 g) goat cheese

• • ● •

Chutney: Sprinkle eggplant with salt and let stand for 10 minutes to draw off bitter juices. In a heavy skillet, heat oil. Over medium heat, sauté onions and garlic until tender, about 5 to 6 minutes. Add maple syrup, jelly, wine and vinegar. Cook, uncovered, until slightly thickened, about 3 to 4 minutes. Add eggplant and chives; cook, covered, for about 5 minutes. Season with salt and pepper. Refrigerate until ready to serve.

Arrange salad greens on chilled plates and place 4 to 6 eggplant slices on each. Top with some cheese and drizzle with remaining cooking liquid from eggplant. Garnish cheese with a salad green sprig.

• • ● •

SERVES 6

Recipe by chef Leo Pantel
Photography: Patricia Holdsworth

Pair With:
• Mission Hill Pinot Noir
• Stoneleigh Marlborough Sauvignon Blanc
• Les Foundettes Sancerre

Charred Romaine with Caesar's Revenge Dressing & Grilled Garlic Croûtons

A rasp is essential to this recipe – it can reduce garlic cloves to a fine paste.

Caesar's Revenge Dressing:
3 egg yolks
1 tbsp (15 mL) anchovy paste
2-3 large garlic cloves, grated
pinch of sea salt
1 1/2 tsp (7 mL) lemon juice
1 tbsp (15 mL) Dijon mustard
1 tsp (5 mL) Worcestershire sauce
2 tsp (10 mL) red wine vinegar
1/2 cup (125 mL) extra-virgin olive oil
1/2 cup (125 mL) grated Asiago cheese
pepper, to taste

Grilled Garlic Croûtons:
1/4 cup (60 mL) butter, softened
1/2 tsp (2 mL) EACH, dried oregano
   and basil
2 garlic cloves, finely minced
salt and pepper, to taste
4 slices of Pumpernickel bread

Charred Romaine:
2 romaine lettuce hearts, rinsed and
   patted dry
2 tbsp (30 mL) olive oil
salt and pepper, to taste

Dressing: In a large bowl, combine egg yolks, anchovy paste, garlic and salt. Whisk well. Pour in lemon juice, mustard, Worcestershire and vinegar; mix vigorously. Slowly pour oil in a thin stream whisking well. Add cheese and season with pepper; mix again. Pour into a container and chill for 1 hour. Shake before serving.

Croûtons: Combine butter, herbs and garlic in a bowl. Season with salt and pepper. Spread over both sides of bread. Preheat a barbecue. When hot, grill bread slices for 30 seconds; turn 45 degrees and cook another 30 seconds, until nicely toasted. Flip and repeat. Remove from heat and cut into 1" (2.5 cm) squares.

Preheat barbecue. Brush romaine with oil. Place on grill and sear for about 2 minutes. Turn and sear on all sides. Remove from heat and remove core; season with salt and pepper. Drizzle with dressing and top with croûtons. Serve immediately.

Recipe by Brandon Boone
Photography: Brian Gould

Pair With:
• Verdicchio
  • B.C. Pinot Blanc
• Perrier

Tomato & Asparagus Salad with Candied Walnuts & Orange Vinaigrette

Orange Vinaigrette:
1/4 cup (60 mL) extra-virgin olive oil
3 tbsp (45 mL) balsamic vinegar
1 tbsp (15 mL) honey
2 tbsp (30 mL) orange juice
1 tsp (5 mL) grated orange zest

Candied Walnuts:
vegetable spray
1 tbsp (15 mL) honey
2 tsp (10 mL) sugar
1/2 cup (125 mL) whole walnuts

Tomato & Asparagus Salad:
8 asparagus spears
romaine OR any green leaf lettuce
freshly shaved Parmesan cheese
4 Roma tomatoes, quartered
salt and pepper to taste

● ● ● ●

Vinaigrette: Combine oil with vinegar and honey; add orange juice, zest and mix well. Cover and let stand for 15 minutes so flavours can blend.

Walnuts: Preheat oven to 325°F (160°C). Spray a baking sheet with vegetable spray. Combine honey and sugar in a small bowl; add walnuts and toss to coat. Spread nuts on baking sheet and bake until honey and sugar mixture is bubbling, about 15 minutes. Cool completely on baking sheet.

Salad: Fill a medium-sized saucepan with water and bring to a boil. Blanch asparagus in boiling water until al dente, about 3 minutes. Remove asparagus from water and cool in ice water. Arrange lettuce leaves on a plate and top with shaved Parmesan. Add tomatoes. Discard asparagus stems and place tips between tomatoes; sprinkle with candied walnuts.

Drizzle Orange Vinaigrette over salad and season with salt and pepper.

● ● ● ●

SERVES 2

Recipe by Andrew Gandier
Photography: Brian Gould

# Quattro Fromaggio Salad

4 Roma tomatoes, sliced into 1/2" (1.3 cm) pieces
4 thin slices of provolone
16 fresh basil leaves
2 oz (60 g) piece of Camembert, cut into 4, 1/2 oz (15 g) wedges
1 cup (250 mL) aged Cheddar, cubed
4 oz (125 g) creamy Greek feta
1/2 cup (125 mL) pomegranate seeds
3/4 cup (175 mL) whole walnuts, toasted
juice of 1/2 an orange
1 tbsp (15 mL) honey
1 tbsp (15 mL) extra-virgin olive oil
salt and pepper, to taste

● ● ● ●

In the centre of each of 4 plates, arrange 5 tomato slices in a single layer. Top with provolone slices, then with fresh basil leaves. Pile Camembert, Cheddar, and feta on top of basil. Sprinkle with pomegranate seeds and walnuts.

In a separate bowl, combine orange juice, honey and oil; season with salt and pepper. Drizzle orange dressing over cheese salad and serve immediately.

● ● ● ●

SERVES 4 AS AN APPETIZER

Recipe by Brandon Boone
Photography: Brian Gould

Pair With:
• White Sancerre
• Australian Riesling
• Austrian Grüner Veltliner

Indian Summer Corn Salad with Chili-Lemon Dressing

Use super-sweet fresh corn and don't omit the smoked cheese; it makes a difference.

2 ears fresh super-sweet corn
2 tbsp (30 mL) diced jalapeños
1/2 cup (125 mL) diced red bell pepper
2/3 cup (150 mL) chopped tomatoes
1/3 cup (75 mL) diced red onion
3 oz (90 g) smoked Gouda cheese
1/3 cup (75 mL) toasted slivered almonds

Chili-Lemon Dressing:
1 tbsp (15 mL) EACH, fresh lemon juice and rice vinegar
2 tbsp (30 mL) olive oil
1/2 tsp (2 mL) chili powder
dash of cayenne pepper
3/4 tsp (4 mL) salt

• • • •

Cut corn kernels off cobs and place in a bowl; add remaining vegetables to corn. Cut cheese into 1/4" (6 mm) cubes and add to corn mixture.

Dressing: In a separate bowl or jar combine all dressing ingredients and whisk or shake well. Just before serving, pour dressing over vegetables and toss. Top with toasted almonds.

• • • •

SERVES 4

Recipe by Craig Guenther
Photography: Brian Gould

Pair With:
• Wyndham Estate Bin 777 Semillon
• Arrowood Viognier
• Sleeman's Cream Ale

Shredded Carrot & Apple Salad with Toasted Almonds

2 large carrots, peeled
1 large apple, peeled
1/2 cup (125 mL) sliced almonds
juice and zest of 1/2 a lemon
1 tbsp (15 mL) honey

• • • •

Grate carrots and apple by hand; place in a medium bowl. Toast sliced almonds in a skillet, over low heat, until golden brown. Add lemon juice and honey to carrots and apple, mixing well. Add almonds and toss gently.

• • • •

SERVES 2

Recipe by chef Stephan Joachim
Photography: Brian Gould

Pair With:
• India Pale Ale
• Canadian Chardonnay
• California Cabernet Sauvignon

Citrus Couscous Salad

Fresh oranges and lemons add zing to this cooling Mediterranean-style salad.

2 red bell peppers
1 jalapeño pepper
2 oranges
1 1/4 cups (300 mL) couscous
2-3 green onions
3 tbsp (45 mL) olive oil
2 tbsp (30 mL) fresh lemon juice
1 garlic clove, minced
3/4 tsp (3 mL) salt
1/2 tsp (2 mL) EACH granulated sugar
   and ground cumin
freshly ground black pepper
1/4 cup (60 mL) dried currants
1/4 cup (60 mL) parsley
1/2 cup (125 mL) pine nuts OR slivered
   almonds, toasted

• • • •

Place whole peppers on a preheated barbecue and sear until all sides are blackened; cool before handling. Peel and seed peppers. Grate zest of 1 orange; set aside. Juice the same orange and add enough water to make 1 1/4 cups (300 mL). Heat liquid to boiling in microwave or in a small saucepan. Pour over couscous in a small bowl; cover and let stand 5 minutes, or until liquid is absorbed.

Peel and section remaining orange; then cut sections into small pieces. Dice bell peppers and very finely dice jalapeño. Thinly slice green onions. In a small bowl, stir oil with 2 tsp (10 mL) grated orange zest, lemon juice, garlic, salt, sugar, cumin and a couple of grindings of black pepper.

Place couscous in a large bowl. Stir in diced peppers, currants, green onions and parsley. Whisk oil mixture; stir into couscous. Cover and chill for a couple of hours if possible, or up to 2 days, so flavours mellow. When serving, stir in orange pieces and nuts. This fruity salad is a great complement to chicken, especially Portuguese grilled chicken with spicy Peri-Peri sauce or hot wings.

• • • •

SERVES 6-8

Recipe by Marilyn Bentz Crowley
Photography: Brian Gould

Pair With:
• Canadian Pinot Gris
• German Riesling
• Californian Pinot Noir

Barley Pecan Salad

A delicious mixture of familiar ingredients.

2 cups (500 mL) quick-cooking barley (or use regular and cook longer)
4 cups (1 L) water
1 tsp (5 mL) salt
4 carrots, finely diced
4 celery stalks, finely diced
1/2 cup (125 mL) chopped fresh dill OR basil
2 shallots, chopped OR 2 green onions, sliced
1/2 cup (125 mL) olive oil
1/4 cup (60 mL) fresh lime OR lemon juice
1/4 tsp (1 mL) EACH salt and freshly ground black pepper
1 1/2 cups (375 mL) chopped toasted pecans
4-6 strips bacon, cooked, crumbled

• • • •

Combine barley, water and salt and bring to a boil. Simmer for 10 minutes. Let stand 5 minutes. (If using regular barley cook according to package directions.) Drain barley; rinse under cold running water and drain again. Toss with vegetables and herbs. Whisk oil with juice, salt and pepper; stir into barley mixture. Taste and add additional seasoning as needed. Chill for a couple of hours or up to 2 days. When ready to serve, stir in pecans and sprinkle with crumbled bacon. The smoky flavour of the bacon will complement barbecued ribs or cheeseburgers.

• • • •

SERVES 6-8

Recipe by Marilyn Bentz Crowley
Photography: Brian Gould

Pair With:
• Canadian Sauvignon Blanc
• Henry of Pelham Cabernet-Merlot
• Fort Garry Dark beer

Wild Rice & Chickpea Salad with Tahini Dressing

The Prairies meet the Middle East, tastefully, in this hearty salad. Or slot in Wehani, a long-grained red rice developed in California and available at natural food stores.

1 cup (250 mL) wild rice
  OR Wehani*
4 cups (1 L) water
1 tsp (5 mL) salt

Tahini Dressing:
1 lemon
2 tbsp (25 mL) tahini
1/4 cup (60 mL) olive oil
2 tbsp (30 mL) water
1 garlic clove, minced
2 tsp (10 mL) dark
  sesame oil
1/2 tsp (5 mL) salt
1/8 tsp (0.5 mL) freshly
  ground black pepper

19 oz (540 mL) can
  chickpeas, drained
2 large carrots, julienned
  or grated
1/2 cup (125 mL) chopped fresh parsley OR coriander
4 large plum tomatoes

• • ● •

Place wild rice into a small saucepan. Add cold water and salt. Bring to a boil. Partially cover and simmer 40 to 45 minutes, or until just tender; then drain. Cool rice.

Dressing: Grate lemon zest; set aside for garnish. Juice lemon. Whisk tahini with oil, 2 tbsp (30 mL) lemon juice, water, garlic, sesame oil, salt and pepper until almost smooth.

Turn cooled rice into a large bowl. Stir in chickpeas, carrots and parsley; then mix in dressing. If serving salad right away, seed and dice tomatoes; stir in. Or cover salad and refrigerate up to 2 days; stir in tomatoes at serving time. Scatter lemon zest over salad. Pairs perfectly with barbecued salmon, trout or shrimp.

* To cook Wehani Rice, wash rice and add 2 cups (500 mL) cold water and 1/2 tsp (2 mL) salt. Bring to a boil over high heat. Cover, reduce heat and simmer 45 minutes. Let sit, covered, off heat, for 10 minutes before fluffing and cooling.

• • ● •

SERVES 6-8

Recipe by Marilyn Bentz Crowley
Photography: Brian Gould

Pair With:
• Chilean Chardonnay
• Canadian Gamay Noir
• Nut Brown Ale

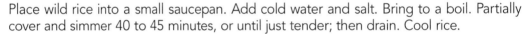

 North African Potato Salad

This lemony potato salad is slightly spicy, yet not so hot that the other flavours are overpowered by the heat. It is characteristic of southern Mediterranean cuisine, featuring the spice mixture of cumin, caraway and cayenne known as harissa.

2-2 1/2 lbs (1-1.25 kg) new potatoes

Harissa:
1 tsp (5 mL) cumin seed
1 tsp (5 mL) caraway seed
1/4 tsp (1 mL) cayenne
1 1/2 tsp (7 mL) salt
3 tbsp (45 mL) fresh lemon juice
1/4 cup (60 mL) olive oil
fresh coriander OR parsley

• • • •

Place potatoes in a large saucepan; generously cover with cold water. Partially cover; bring to a boil over high heat. Reduce heat so water boils gently; cook 20 minutes, or until potatoes are just tender when pierced with a skewer. Drain and cool to touch. Without peeling, cut potatoes into 1" (2.5 cm) chunks.

Harissa: Partially crush cumin and caraway seeds using a mortar and pestle or in a mini food processor. In a small bowl, stir seeds with cayenne, salt and lemon juice. Heat oil in a large skillet over medium-high heat until very hot, but not smoking. Stir lemon juice mixture and carefully pour into hot oil; cook 2 to 3 minutes, or until steaming stops and seeds look darker.

Add potatoes to harissa; using a large spatula, mix well by lifting from the bottom. Cool. Store, covered, in refrigerator for up to 3 days. When ready to serve, garnish with chopped coriander. Delicious as an accompaniment to barbecued turkey and chicken.

• • • •

SERVES 6 TO 8

Recipe by
   Marilyn Bentz Crowley
Photography: Brian Gould

Pair With:
• South African Cabernet Sauvignon
• Chilean Sauvignon Blanc

'Smokin' Gun Mayonnaise

Absolutely perfect as a condiment to top a barbecued cheeseburger.

1/4 cup (60 mL) mayonnaise
2 tsp (10 mL) smoked paprika
2 tsp (10 mL) roasted garlic
1/2 tsp (2 mL) cayenne
1/2 tsp (2 mL) kosher salt

● ● ● ●

Combine all ingredients in a small bowl and mix until blended.
Refrigerate, covered, until ready to use.

● ● ● ●

Recipe by Brandon Boone
Photography: Brian Gould

Berberé Yogurt Spread

This spice mix may seem like a lot of trouble, but it is worth it. Use some for the yogurt spread and save the rest for a million other uses such as a rub on roast chicken or seasoning for roasted potatoes. Use this spread on sandwiches, burgers or crackers, and as a crudité dip.

Berberé Spice Mix:
1 tbsp (15 mL) cumin seeds
4 whole cloves
1 tsp (5 mL) EACH, cardamom seeds, peppercorns, fenugreek seeds, coriander seeds, fennel seeds
1 tsp (5 mL) dried chile flakes (more if you like heat)
1 tsp (5 mL) ginger powder
1 tbsp (15 mL) coarse salt
1/2 tsp (2 mL) cinnamon
1/4 cup (60 mL) EACH, brown sugar and paprika

Yogurt Spread:
3 cups (750 mL) low-fat yogurt
1/4 cup (60 mL) honey
1 tbsp (15 mL) Berberé spice mix, or more to taste

• • • •

Spice Mix: In a skillet over medium heat, toast whole spices, stirring constantly. Cook for 2 minutes then transfer to a spice grinder (a clean coffee grinder or mortar and pestle will crush the spices). Process whole spices until ground; combine with remaining ingredients. Store in an airtight jar until ready to use.

Spread: Line a colander with cheesecloth and place in a bowl. Pour yogurt into colander. Put a small plate on top and let yogurt drain in the fridge overnight. Combine honey and spice mix with thickened yogurt; mix well.

• • • •

Recipe by chef Alex Svenne
Photography: Brian Gould

egetable Ketchup

Try this big-flavour spread as a condiment for burgers, steaks, roast beef or sandwiches.

12 Roma tomatoes
2 large carrots
1 onion, peeled
4 garlic cloves
1 red pepper
2 apples, cored, quartered and cut
   into chunks
1 tbsp (15 mL) canola oil
salt and pepper
5.5 oz (156 mL) can tomato paste
1/2 cup (125 mL) vinegar
1/2 cup (125 mL brown sugar
1 cup (250 mL) water

• • • •

Preheat oven to 375°F (190°C). Cut vegetables into big chunks. Toss vegetables and apple with canola oil to coat; spread on a cookie sheet. Season with salt and pepper. Roast vegetables until very tender (they may start to blacken, this is OK). Remove from heat and let cool slightly. Working in batches, purée vegetables in a blender or food processor until smooth; strain purée through a mesh sieve or a food mill into a large pot. Combine remaining ingredients with purée and bring to a boil; reduce heat to a simmer and cook until the purée has the consistency of ketchup.

• • • •

Recipe by chef Alex Svenne
Photography: Brian Gould

ot Tomato Jam

This really kicks up grilled cheese. Or, pile it on a roast beef sandwich with a healthy dollop of horseradish.

1 tbsp (15 mL) olive oil
1 large onion, diced
1 large garlic clove, diced
1 tbsp (15 mL) dried chile peppers
1 tsp (5 mL) coriander seeds
 28 oz (796 mL) can diced tomatoes
1/2 cup (125 mL) white wine
1 cup (250 mL) water
1/2 cup (125 mL) brown sugar

• • ■ •

Heat oil in a skillet over medium heat and sauté onion until golden brown. Add garlic, chiles, coriander, tomatoes and white wine to the skillet and bring to a boil. Reduce heat to medium and let mixture reduce until almost dry. Add water and brown sugar, mixing with other ingredients, and reduce until jam-like consistency.

• • ■ •

Recipe by chef Alex Svenne

pricot Chutney

Great on a grilled chicken sandwich or mixed into egg salad.

1 tbsp (15 mL) canola oil
1 small onion, finely diced
1 red bell pepper, finely diced
1 tbsp (15 mL) grated ginger
1 tsp (5 mL) dried chile flakes
1 cup (250 g) chopped dried apricots
1/2 cup (125 mL) brown sugar
1 cup (250 mL) orange juice
1/2 cup (125 mL) white vinegar

• • ■ •

Heat oil in a skillet over medium heat; sauté onion and pepper until tender and starting to brown. Add remaining ingredients; cook until reduced to jam-like consistency.

• • ■ •

Recipe by chef Alex Svenne

Big Bang Barbecue Rub

Try this magic seasoning on chicken legs, breasts or whole chickens. Sprinkle or rub over whatever you're making and let sit, covered, for about an hour.

2 tbsp (30 mL) smoked paprika
1 tbsp (15 mL) paprika
1 tbsp (15 mL) onion powder
1 tbsp (15 mL) kosher salt
1 tsp (5 mL) freshly cracked black peppercorns
1 tbsp (15 mL) dry mustard
1 tsp (5 mL) brown sugar
2 garlic cloves, minced
1 1/2 tsp (7 mL) chili powder
1 tsp (5 mL) cayenne

● ● ● ●

Combine all ingredients, making sure to break up any lumps. Store in an airtight container.

● ● ● ●

Recipe by Brandon Boone

Photography: Brian Gould

Pair With:
• St. Hubertus Pinot Blanc
• Sterling Vineyards Chardonnay
• Miller Genuine Draft

Juniper's Union Rub

Look for juniper berries in the bulk section of your local health food store. Crushing the berries releases their gin-like flavour. Often overlooked, these berries harmonize beautifully with the flavour of ostrich, duck or game hen.

3 tbsp (45 mL) juniper berries
1 1/2 tsp (7 mL) peppercorns
1 tsp (5 mL) ground allspice
1 tbsp (15 mL) brown sugar
1 tsp (5 mL) kosher salt
1 tsp (5 mL) crumbled dried rosemary
1 tsp (5 mL) ground dried orange peel (can substitute orange zest)

● ● ● ●

Toast berries and peppercorns in a small skillet, about 5 to 6 minutes, to bring out flavour. Remove from pan and let cool. When cooled, grind berries and peppercorns with a mortar and pestle or in a mini chopper. In a small bowl, mix ground berries and peppercorns with remaining ingredients. Store in an airtight container.

● ● ● ●

Recipe by Brandon Boone
Photography: Brian Gould

Pair With:
• Californian Cabernet Sauvignon
• Gin and tonic
• Chilean Merlot

Devil-May-Care Rub

Not for the faint of heart. This is a wet version of a spice rub. Use on pork ribs, steaks or bison. Works very well as a coating for whole beef roasts.

1 dried chipotle pepper OR 1 chipotle pepper in adobo sauce, chopped
2 tbsp (30 mL) minced garlic
1/4 cup (60 mL) packed brown sugar
3 tbsp (45 mL) balsamic vinegar
2 tsp (10 mL) hot pepper flakes
1/4 cup (60 mL) tomato paste
1 tbsp (15 mL) hot pepper sauce
2 tsp (10 mL) kosher salt
1 tsp (5 mL) ground dried lemon grass OR grated lemon zest

• • • •

Grind chipotle pepper. Place ground chipotle and remaining ingredients in a bowl; mix well. Store in the refrigerator, covered.

• • • •

Recipe by Brandon Boone

Photography: Brian Gould

Pair With:
• Rum and cola
• Honey Brown Lager
• Australian Shiraz

Green Beans with Golden Shallot & Thyme Compound Butter

Place a thick coin of this scrumptious butter on pork chops or green beans for an instant sauce.

Golden Shallot & Thyme Compound Butter:

2 medium shallots

1 tbsp (15 mL) canola OR olive oil

1/2 cup (250 mL) softened salted butter

2 tsp (10 mL) chopped fresh thyme OR 1/2 tsp (2 mL) dried leaves

2 cups (500 mL) trimmed green beans

● ● ● ●

Butter: Finely mince shallots. Heat oil in a small skillet over medium-low heat until hot. Add shallots; fry for 4 to 5 minutes, stirring often, or until golden. Remove from heat and let cool. Stir butter with a fork in a small bowl; work in shallots and thyme. Spoon onto parchment or waxed paper; roll up to form a log about 1" (2.5 cm) thick. Refrigerate for up to a week or freeze. Cut butter into coins about 1/2" (1.3 cm) thick.

Steam green beans over gentle simmering water for 5 to 7 minutes, or until tender. Remove from heat and top with a few slices of Compound Butter.

● ● ● ●

MAKES 1/2 CUP (125 ML) COMPOUND BUTTER

Variations: Replace thyme with basil and work in 3 to 4 finely minced sun-dried tomatoes; toss flavoured butter with hot pasta for an instant sauce. Or work 2 tbsp (30 mL) crumbled Roquefort or Danish Blue cheese into flavoured butter; chill. Top a grilled steak with a thick coin and serve with a side of pomme frites for a classic combination.

Recipe by Marilyn Bentz Crowley

Photography: Brian Gould

Pair With:
• Verdicchio
• Vihno Verde
• B.C. Pinot Blanc

Buttery Stir-fry of Pea Shoots with Baby Peas & Radishes

1 tsp (5 mL) cold-pressed canola oil
1/4 cup (60 mL) butter
2 cups (500 mL) frozen tiny peas, rinsed in cold water
3 green onions, white part only, sliced on diagonal
6 small red radishes, quartered
1 cup (250 mL) packed young pea shoots
salt and pepper, to taste

• • • •

Heat a skillet to medium-hot. Add oil and melt butter in oil. Add peas, onions and radishes and stir-fry 1 minute. Rinse pea shoots in cold water; shake dry and add to pan. Turn quickly for 30 seconds, until just coated with butter. Add salt and a good grinding of black pepper. Serve as a side dish to roast chicken with a mesclun salad tossed with a handful of fresh sprouts, dressed with roasting juices and a bit of your chosen wine.

• • • •

SERVES 4

Recipe by Judy Schultz
Photography: John Ulan/Epic Photography

Pair With:
• Villa Girardi Terre Lunghe
• Cedar Creek Pinot Gris
• Tasca D'Almerita Regaleali Rosato

Root Vegetable Fries with Southwest Seasoning

1 large yellow potato
1 yam
1 parsnip
1 large beet
1 jicama
1 tbsp (15 mL) coarse salt
1 tbsp (15 mL) cumin seeds, toasted and crushed
1 tbsp (15 mL) chili powder
1 tsp (5 mL) chipotle* pepper OR cayenne
1/4 cup (60 mL) shelled pepitas (pumpkin seeds), toasted and crushed
canola oil for deep-frying
1 lime
1 tbsp (15 mL) chopped cilantro

• • • •

Peel and julienne vegetables. In a bowl, combine salt, spices and pepitas. In a large pot or deep fryer, heat oil to 350°F (180°C). Add julienned vegetables, except beets, to oil and fry until crisp. Remove from oil and let drain. Add beets and fry until soft. Remove from oil and let drain. Drizzle with lime juice and sprinkle with salt mixture and cilantro. Serve immediately.

* smoked jalapeños, dried and ground into a powder

• • • •

SERVES 4

Recipe by chef Alex Svenne
Photography: Brian Gould

Pair With:
• Cream Ale
• Orvieto
• Rootbeer

Jamaican Rice & Peas

In Jamaica, beans such as kidney beans are often referred to as peas.

1/4 cup (60 mL) dried kidney beans
2 cups (500 mL) rice
2 cups (500 mL) water
2 green onions, chopped
1 garlic clove, crushed
pinch of black pepper, or to taste
1 tsp (5 mL) thyme
1/4 cup (60 mL) unsweetened coconut milk

• • • •

Pick over beans to remove any dirt or debris. Place beans in a medium saucepan, add water to cover and soak for 3 hours. Bring beans to a boil, reduce heat and simmer approximately 35 minutes, until beans are tender. Add rice, water and all other ingredients to pot. Use a fork to distribute ingredients evenly (using care not to break up beans) and return to a boil. Cover, reduce heat to low and simmer, without lifting lid, for 15 minutes. Remove from heat and let stand, covered, for 5 minutes before serving.

• • • •

SERVES 6-8

Recipe by Don Woodstock
Photography: Brian Gould

Pair With:
• Pale Ale
• Valpolicella
• Beaujolais Villages

Thai New Potatoes

Thai flavours, especially fresh ginger, add an innovative dimension to new potatoes.

2 lbs (1 kg) small new potatoes
1 tbsp (15 mL) salt, preferably sea OR coarse salt
cold water to cover
1 small hot red pepper OR pinches of cayenne
3 tbsp (45 mL) canola OR olive oil
1 tsp (5 mL) dark sesame oil
2 tbsp (30 mL) grated fresh ginger
1/4 tsp (1 mL) salt
1/4 cup (60 mL) EACH, fresh mint and coriander OR flat-leaf parsley
2 green onions, thinly sliced

● ● ● ●

Scrub potatoes, but do not peel or pierce. Place in a large kettle; add salt and generously cover with cold water. Don't cheat with hot water or potatoes may crack. Bring to a boil over high heat; reduce heat to a gentle boil for 15 to 25 minutes, depending on size of potatoes. When tender, drain. Cut into 1" (2.5 cm) chunks. Potatoes can be covered and refrigerated for up to 2 days.

Seed and finely dice red pepper; taste a tiny piece to decide on the "heat" level, fiery to mild. Heat oils in a large skillet over medium-high heat. Add potatoes; cook 10 to 15 minutes, shaking pan frequently, until potatoes are hot and starting to brown. Stir in ginger and salt; cook 30 to 60 seconds. Then sprinkle with coriander, mint, green onions and some or all of minced red pepper; shake pan until herbs are wilted and potatoes are coated. Serve immediately with grilled pork steaks or chops.

● ● ● ●

SERVES 6-8

Recipe by Marilyn Bentz Crowley
Photography: Brian Gould

Pair With:
• Gewürztraminer
• Sander Weissburgunder
• Lingenfelder Riesling

(S)hore Salt Potatoes

Clambake potatoes are boiled in seawater, resulting in tender skins filmed with salt and with incredibly creamy interiors. Salt potatoes are easy to reproduce far inland, however, don't think about reducing the amount of salt below as the cooked potatoes emerge perfectly seasoned, not salty.

2 lbs (1 kg) tiny to extra-small new potatoes
1/4 cup (60 mL) kosher OR sea salt
cold water to cover
1/2 lb (250 g) butter, melted

• • • •

Scrub potatoes, but do not peel or pierce. Turn into a large kettle or pot; add salt and generously cover with cold water. Don't skimp on the hot water or potatoes may crack during boiling. Bring to a boil over high heat; then reduce heat to a gentle boil for 15 to 20 minutes, depending on size of potatoes. When tender, drain and serve immediately with melted butter for dipping. Serve with Italian sausages snappy-crisp from the grill, steamed clams or mussels – or all three for a seashore feast.

• • • •

SERVES 6-8

Recipe by Marilyn Bentz Crowley
Photography: Brian Gould

Pair With:
• Australian Shiraz
• Canadian Pinot Gris
• India Pale Ale

MAIN DISHES

Pasta
Seafood
Poultry
Lamb
Pork
Veal
Beef

resh Pasta Dough

1 cup (250 mL) cake flour
1/4 cup (60 mL) whole-wheat flour, add more as necessary
3 large eggs
2 tbsp (30 mL) olive oil
1 tbsp (15 mL) water
pinch of kosher salt

In the mixing bowl of a stand mixer, combine all ingredients. Using the dough hook, mix all ingredients until they form a ball shape. Add additional flour as needed. Remove dough from bowl and knead on a lightly floured surface for 5 to 10 minutes, or until smooth and elastic. Wrap dough in plastic wrap and let rest for 1 hour.

When ready to use, divide dough into 4 equal portions. Cover 3 portions with plastic wrap until ready to use. Stretch 1 piece into a rectangle. Place pasta machine roller on highest setting and feed pasta dough through. Continue to roll pasta dough through 2 or 3 more times. Reduce the rolling machine by one setting and pass dough through. Continue the process until you reach the desired thickness. If cutting into narrow lengths, select the appropriate cutters on the machine and pass dough through. Bring a pot of salted water to boil and cook pasta to desired tenderness.

Recipe by Brandon Boone
Photography: Brian Gould

Fresh Sage Ravioli Stuffed with Sweet Potato in a Brown Butter Sauce

Ravioli:
I recipe Fresh Pasta Dough, page 126, with 2 1/2 tbsp (37 mL) minced fresh sage added during the mixing 2 lbs (1 kg) sweet potatoes
1/2 cup (75 mL) plain yogurt
1 1/2 tbsp (22 mL) minced fresh chives
1 egg beaten with 1 tbsp (15 mL) water

Brown Butter Sauce:
2 tbsp (30 mL) unsalted butter
3 tbsp (45 mL) chopped walnuts
1/3 cup (75 mL) chopped shallots
2 garlic cloves, minced
1/2 cup (125 mL) white wine
3/4 cup (175 mL) whipping cream
2 tbsp (30 mL) chopped fresh parsley
Asiago cheese for garnish

Ravioli: Prepare dough. Preheat oven to 375°F (190°C). Cut sweet potatoes in half and place cut side down on an oiled baking pan. Bake for 40 to 50 minutes, or until tender. Remove from oven and spoon out 1 1/2 cups (375 mL) of potato flesh. Let cool to room temperature. In a bowl, combine sweet potato, yogurt and chives; mix until well blended. Season with salt and pepper.

Divide pasta dough into 4 balls. Working with 1 at a time; cover the rest while not in use. Roll pasta dough to roughly 1/2" (1.3 cm) thick and no wider than the pasta machine. Roll dough through the machine's highest setting. If you don't have a pasta roller, you can simply use a rolling pin. If so, roll until dough is about 1/8" (3 mm) thick.

If using a pasta machine, continue to roll dough through machine, moving down one setting each time until desired thickness. Repeat with remaining balls of dough. Using a cookie cutter, cut dough into 3" (8 cm) circles. Or, cut into 3" (8 cm) squares.

Place 2 tsp (10 mL) filling in the centre of each piece. Using a pastry brush, brush 1/2 of the outside edge of pasta with egg wash and fold over to seal. Repeat with remaining dough. Boil ravioli in a pot of salted water for about 3 to 5 minutes, or until cooked.

Sauce: In a skillet over medium heat, melt butter; add walnuts and stir until deep brown and fragrant. Remove from pan with a slotted spoon. Add shallots and garlic and sauté for about 1 minute, or until softened. Add wine and cream; bring to a boil and reduce by half. Add cooked ravioli to pan and toss to coat. Divide among 4 plates and top with parsley, walnuts and Asiago cheese. Serve immediately.

SERVES 4

Recipe by Brandon Boone

Photography: Brian Gould

Pair With:
• Italian Arneis
• Vintage Sake
• Australian Chardonnay

Linguine with Lemon Butter

As Italian children know, the best nursery food of all is pasta simply tossed with butter and cheese. Here's an adult version with hits of lemon and chile.

8 oz (250 g) dry linguine OR fettuccine
1 large lemon
1 tbsp (15 mL) olive oil
1 medium onion
2 large garlic cloves, minced
1 tsp (5 mL) crushed chile flakes
1/4 cup (60 mL) salted butter, cut into equal slices
1 cup (250 mL) freshly grated Parmigiano Reggiano
3 green onions, thinly sliced
freshly ground black pepper

● ● ● ●

Prepare pasta accordingly to manufacturer's suggestions. Grate lemon zest and squeeze juice. Heat oil in a large skillet over medium heat; add onion, garlic and chile flakes. Sauté 2 to 3 minutes, or until softened. Add lemon zest and 1/4 cup (60 mL) lemon juice; simmer 1 minute. Remove pan from heat and slowly stir in butter. Sauce should be thick and creamy. Set aside if ready before the pasta. Add drained pasta to lemon mixture in pan; return to heat. Using tongs, mix well. Toss with Parmesan cheese, green onions and several grindings of black pepper. Serve immediately with extra grated cheese and crushed chile flakes on the side.

● ● ● ●

SERVES 4

Recipe by Marilyn Bentz Crowley
Photography: Brian Gould

Pair With:
• Loire Valley Sauvignon Blanc
• Margaret River Sauvignon Semillon
• German Kabinett Riesling

Angel Hair Pasta with Asparagus & Snow Goat Cheese

1 bunch of green asparagus
handful of cleaned fiddleheads (optional)
1 tsp (5 mL) extra-virgin olive oil
1/4 cup (60 mL) butter
1 garlic clove, halved
2 tbsp (30 mL) of the wine you've chosen
1/2 cup (125 mL) whipping cream, room temperature
8 oz (250 g) dry angel hair pasta
8 oz (250 g) snow goat cheese (fresh mild chèvre)
salt and pepper, to taste
1/4 cup (60 mL) chopped fresh flat-leaf parsley

● ● ○ ●

Wash asparagus and trim stems where they snap off naturally. Cut in thirds, length-wise. If using fiddleheads, rinse under cold water, removing papery brown husk.

In a large skillet, heat oil and melt butter in oil over medium heat. Add garlic. Sauté until golden. Remove garlic and discard. Add wine, and let sauce cook a bit. Add asparagus, tossing just to coat; add cream and bring to a simmer.

Bring a large pot of salted water to a boil. Add pasta and cook until barely al dente, 3 to 5 minutes. Drain pasta and immediately add to pan with asparagus sauce. Pinch off pieces of chèvre and add to pasta, tossing as you do so. Add salt and pepper. Add parsley; toss and serve immediately in warmed pasta plates.

● ● ○ ●

SERVES 4

Recipe by Judy Schultz
Photography: John Ulan/Epic Photography

Pair With:
• Californian Sauvignon Blanc
• Italian Soave

Cracked Black Pepper Orecchiette with Asparagus, Pine Nuts & Sultanas

One wouldn't normally think to add raisins, or in this case sultanas, to a pasta recipe but the flavour they impart makes the whole dish sing.

1 recipe Fresh Pasta Dough, page 126, with
   1 tbsp (15 mL) freshly cracked black pepper added before mixing
1 lb (500 g) fresh asparagus, trimmed and cut into 3" (8 cm) pieces
1/4 cup (60 mL) pine nuts
1/4 cup (60 mL) olive oil
3 garlic cloves, minced
1 purple onion, sliced
grated zest and juice of 1 lemon
1/4 cup (60 mL) sultanas
salt, to taste
freshly grated Parmesan cheese for garnish

● ● ● ●

Orecchiette: Divide dough into 4 portions. Roll each into a log, about 1/2" (1.3 cm) in diameter. Cut log into 1/8" (3 mm) pieces and press each piece between index finger and thumb to form pasta "ears." Repeat with remaining pieces. Lay orecchiette on a dishtowel until ready to use. When ready to cook, bring a pot of salted water to a boil; add orecchiette and cook for 3 to 4 minutes or until al dente. Drain and keep warm.

Place asparagus in a steamer and cook for about 6 minutes, or until soft but not limp.

In a skillet over medium-low heat, toast pine nuts until lightly browned. Remove from pan and reserve. Heat oil in skillet and add garlic; cook over medium-low heat until fragrant. Add onion and cook until softened. Add lemon zest, juice, asparagus, pine nuts, sultanas and pasta to skillet. Toss to coat; season with salt. Divide among 4 pasta bowls and top with Parmesan.

● ● ● ●

SERVES 4

Recipe by Brandon Boone
Photography: Brian Gould

Pair With:
• Italian Verdicchio
• B.C. Ehrenfelser
• Austrian Gruner Veltliner

(P)asta Poverino

Broccoli, Artichoke and Pepper Sauce:
1 tbsp (15 mL) olive oil
1/2 tsp (5 mL) crushed garlic
1/2 cup (125 mL) small broccoli florets
1/4 cup (60 mL) chopped sun-dried tomatoes
1/4 cup (60 mL) chopped marinated artichoke hearts
1/4 cup (60 mL) EACH, chopped green and red bell peppers
pinch EACH, salt and pepper

1 1/2 cups (375 mL) cooked fusilli pasta
parsley sprigs for garnish

• • ◦ •

Sauce: Heat oil in a skillet over high heat to hot but not smoking. Add garlic. When garlic is golden, add vegetables and sauté until tender.

Divide pasta between 2 plates. Spoon sauce over pasta and garnish with parsley.

• • ◦ •

SERVES 2

Recipe by chef Peter Tudda
Photography: Patricia Holdsworth

Pair With:
• Italian Verdicchio
• B.C. Pinot Blanc
• California Sauvignon Blanc

Fresh Basil Fettuccine with Cherry Tomato, Spinach & Porcini Mushrooms in a White Wine Butter Sauce

1 recipe of Fresh Pasta Dough, page 126, with 3 tbsp (45 mL) minced fresh basil added before mixing, cut into fettuccine

Butter Sauce:
1 tbsp (15 mL) olive oil
1/2 cup (125 mL) unsalted butter, divided
8 oz (250 g) porcini mushrooms, sliced
3 garlic cloves, minced
1/2 cup (125 mL) white wine
1 1/2 cups (375 mL) fresh baby spinach, stems removed
3/4 cup (175 mL) cherry tomatoes
salt and freshly ground pepper, to taste
Asiago cheese

● ● ● ●

Prepare fettuccine.

Sauce: In a skillet over medium-high heat, combine oil and 1 tbsp (15 mL) butter; when butter melts, add mushrooms and sauté until browned. Reduce heat to medium and add garlic; cook for 2 to 3 minutes, stirring frequently. Deglaze pan with wine, stirring up any brown bits on bottom of pan. Let wine reduce by half. Add spinach, tomatoes and 1 tbsp (15 mL) butter, stirring frequently. Add remaining butter in equal portions, stirring after each addition. When all butter has been added and melted, season sauce with salt and pepper.

Toss with fettuccine and serve immediately with a dusting of fresh Asiago.

● ● ● ●

SERVES 4

Recipe by Brandon Boone
Photography: Brian Gould

Pair With:
• Italian Soave Classico
• B.C. Chardonnay
• French White Burgundy

Fettuccine with Valentino Sauce

Valentino Sauce:
1/2 cup (125 mL) butter
3 oz (90 g) pancetta, diced
3 oz (90 g) prosciutto, diced
1 cup (250 mL) sliced mushrooms
1/2 cup (125 mL) chopped white onion
1 tsp (5 mL) chopped garlic
1/2 tsp (2 mL) pepper
1/4 cup (60 mL) flour
3 cups (750 mL) whipping cream
12 oz (341 mL) can of tomato sauce

1 package fettuccine

• • • •

Sauce: In a large pot, melt butter over medium heat. Add pancetta, prosciutto, mushrooms, onion, garlic and pepper; sauté for 7 to 10 minutes. Add flour to the sauce, stirring quickly. Pour in cream and increase heat until sauce begins to simmer, stirring continuously to avoid lumps. Reduce heat to low and add tomato sauce; mix well, cover and simmer for 10 minutes.

Bring a large pot of water to a boil and cook pasta according to manufacturer's instructions. Drain pasta and keep warm until ready to use. Spoon sauce over pasta and serve immediately.

• • • •

MAKES ABOUT 4 1/2 CUPS (1 L) OF SAUCE
    (1 lb/500 g dried pasta serves 4 to 5 as a main course)

Recipe by Dean Petrillo
Photography: John Ulan/Epic Photography

Pair With:
• Italian Rosado
• Spanish Rioja Rosé
• French Tavel

Penne with Rosemary & Pancetta

2 tbsp (30 ml) olive oil
8 oz (250 g) pancetta, sliced thickly and diced
1 medium onion, chopped
2 garlic cloves, chopped
1/2 cup (125 ml) red wine
2 lbs (1 kg) peeled tomatoes, canned or fresh
3 sprigs rosemary
2 lb (1 kg) pkg penne pasta
salt and red pepper flakes to taste
3 oz (90 g) Parmesan cheese

● ● ● ●

Heat oil in a large pot over medium heat; add pancetta, onion and garlic. Cook until pancetta is browned and onion is translucent. Add wine and reduce. Add tomatoes and 1 sprig of rosemary; cook on medium-high for 10 to 15 minutes.

Cook pasta in a large pot of boiling salted water with 1 sprig of rosemary until slightly firmer than al dente. Drain pasta and then add to sauce, adding salt and pepper to taste. Simmer for 1 minute, remove from heat and sprinkle with Parmesan. Use the remaining rosemary sprig to garnish.

● ● ● ●

SERVES 8

Recipe by Beatrice Carlani
Photography: Hamid Attie Photography

Pair With:
• Italian Chianti
• California Pinot Noir
• B.C. Sangiovese

Angelic Tiger Prawn, Bay Scallop & Snow Pea Pasta with Pernod Cream Sauce

1 cup (250 mL) fresh snow peas
5 oz (140 g) angel hair pasta

Pernod Cream Sauce:
1/4 cup (60 mL) butter
6 garlic cloves, minced
1 cup (250 mL) diced white onion
1 oz (30 mL) Pernod liqueur
8 large tiger prawns
8 large bay scallops
1 cup (250 mL) whipping cream
2 tbsp (30 mL) fresh basil chiffonade (thin strips)

● ● ◦ ◦

Fill a large pot with water and bring to a boil. Before preparing pasta, blanch snow peas in boiling water. Remove peas and shock in a bowl of cold water; reserve peas. Cook pasta according to package instructions.

Sauce: Melt butter in a large pan over medium heat. Add garlic and onions to pan and sauté until translucent. Add Pernod; ignite and continue to cook until flame subsides. Add prawns and scallops, cook until tender, about 3 minutes. Add cream and basil and simmer to reduce sauce.

Divide pasta between 2 pasta bowls, drizzle with sauce and top with snow peas.

● ● ◦ ◦

SERVES 2

Recipe by Julian Scott & Andrew Gandier
Photography: Brian Gould

Pair With:
• Grey Monk Riesling

Honey Mushroom & Scallop Pasta

1 lb (500 g) angel hair OR other pasta

Honey Mushroom and Scallop Sauce:
2 tbsp (30 mL) extra-virgin olive oil
1 large white onion, diced
3 garlic cloves, minced
2 cups (500 mL) sliced, blanched honey OR oyster mushrooms
1/2 EACH, red, yellow, green and orange bell peppers, juliennned
3 cups (750 mL) tomato sauce
1/2 cup (125 mL) red OR white wine
1 tbsp (15 mL) chopped fresh oregano
2 tsp (10 mL) chopped fresh thyme
2 tsp (10 mL) chopped fresh marjoram
1 1/2 lbs (750 g) large scallops, rinsed
1/4 cup (60 mL) finely sliced green onions

● ● ○ ○

Cook pasta in boiling salted water following package instructions.

In a skillet over medium-high heat, heat oil and sauté onion until translucent; add garlic and sauté 2 to 3 minutes. Add mushrooms and peppers; reduce heat and cook gently, stirring often, for 5 to 7 minutes. Add tomato sauce, wine and herbs; simmer until slightly thickened. Add scallops and toss with sauce; cover and cook 2 minutes, depending on size of scallops used.

Divide pasta among 4 plates; top with sauce and sprinkle with green onions. Serve with garlic toast.

● ● ○ ○

SERVES 4

Recipe by George Myketa
Photography: Brian Gould

Pair With:
• Jagermeister
• Escudo Rojo
• Fort Garry Pale Ale

Linguine Pescatore

1 1/2 cups (375 mL) cooked linguine

Pescatore Sauce:
1 tbsp (15 mL) olive oil
4 oz (115 g) clams
4 oz (115 g) scallops
4 oz (115 g) shrimp
8 mussels
1 tsp (5 mL) minced fresh garlic
1 cup (250 mL) tomato sauce
parsley sprigs for garnish

● ● ● ●

Prepare linguine.

Sauce: In a skillet over medium-high heat, add oil and seafood to pan. After a couple of minutes, add garlic. Once seafood has become opaque and the mussels have opened (discarding any that haven't), add tomato sauce. Remove from heat and pour over pasta. Place mussels upright around the plate and garnish with parsley sprigs.

● ● ● ●

SERVES 2

Recipe by chef Peter Tudda
Photography: Brian Gould

Pair With:
• Italian Pinot Grigio
• French White Rhone
• New Zealand Sauvignon Blanc

ockles & Mussels

I lb (500 g) mussels
I lb (500 g) clams
1/4 cup (60 mL) butter
1/4 cup (60 mL) finely chopped shallots
freshly ground pepper
1/2 cup (125 mL) dry white wine
1/2 cup (125 mL) chopped flat-leaf parsley
sea salt
lemon wedges for garnish

● ● ● ●

Soak shellfish in water for a few hours, changing the water often. Scrub and de-beard
mussels. Melt butter in a saucepan; add shallots, pepper and wine; simmer, covered,
for 2 to 3 minutes stirring occasionally. Add mussels and clams; cook, covered, for
5 to 7 minutes. Discard any that haven't opened. Divide clams and mussels between
2 bowls. Continue to cook the remaining liquid in the pan until reduced by 1/3; strain
liquid and pour over clams and mussels. Dust with parsley and salt; serve with lemon
wedges.

● ● ● ●

SERVES 2

Recipe by Dave Abbott

Photography: Hamid Attie Photography

Pair With:
• California Sauvignon Blanc
• B.C. White Meritage
• Oregon Pinot Gris

Seared Scallops with a Citrus Drizzle

Citrus Drizzle:
3 navel oranges
2 lemons
2 limes
1 red pepper, finely diced
1/4 cup (60 mL) chopped
  cilantro
1/2 cup (125 mL) orange
  juice
1/3 cup (75 mL) cranberry
  juice
1 tbsp (15 mL) serrano oil
salt and pepper to taste

6 large fresh scallops
salt and pepper, to taste
1/4 cup (60 mL) olive oil
1 head of raddichio
fresh sage leaves

● ● ○ ●

Citrus Drizzle: Peel citrus fruit and discard skin and seeds. Place fruit in a small pot. Add remaining ingredients and bring to a boil; reduce heat and simmer for 5 minutes. Strain through a sieve and refrigerate liquid.

Preheat oven to 450°F (230°C). Season scallops with salt and pepper. Heat oil in a large skillet over medium-high heat; add scallops and sear until golden on both sides. Remove from skillet and bake in oven for 5 minutes; remove from heat and keep warm.

To serve, open raddichio to form a small bowl and place in the centre of a small dinner plate. Top with scallops, drizzle with 2 tbsp (30 mL) of the Citrus Drizzle and garnish with sage leaves.

● ● ○ ●

SERVES 2

Recipe by chef Richard Duncan

Photography: Brian Gould

Pair With:
• Italian Arneis
• Washington State Semillon
• White Bordeaux

Seared Tiger Prawns with Fried Eggplant & Roasted Red Pepper Sauce

4 red bell peppers, roasted, peeled
olive oil for brushing peppers
1/4 cup (60 mL) crème fraîche* OR use recipe on next page
juice of 1 lemon
1 pinch chipotle** powder
1 cup (250 mL) olive oil
salt and pepper, to taste

Fried Eggplant:
1 large eggplant
1/2 cup (125 mL) white flour
salt and pepper, to taste
2 eggs, beaten
1 cup (250 mL) bread crumbs
pinch cayenne pepper
grapeseed oil for frying

Seared Tiger Prawns:
grapeseed oil for frying
6 large tiger prawns
salt and pepper, to taste

● ● ● ●

Sauce: Preheat oven to 375°F (190°C). Place red peppers skin side-up on a lined baking sheet. Using a pastry brush, coat each pepper with oil. Place in oven and roast 30 to 40 minutes, or until skins start to pull away. Remove from oven and place in a glass bowl. Cover with plastic wrap and let cool. When cool, remove skins from peppers.

Place roasted red peppers, crème fraîche, lemon juice and chipotle powder in a blender. With blender still running, slowly add oil in a slow, steady stream to emulsify. Process until smooth. Season with salt and pepper.

Eggplant: Slice eggplant crosswise into 1/4" (6 mm) disks. Dredge in flour seasoned with salt and pepper and tap off excess. Dip in egg and then in bread crumbs seasoned with cayenne pepper. Pan-fry in hot oil until golden brown on both sides.

S eared Tiger Prawns with Fried Eggplant & Roasted Red Pepper Sauce *(continued)*

Prawns: Heat oil in a skillet over medium-high heat. Season prawns with salt and pepper and sear on both sides until just cooked through.

Ladle red pepper sauce onto 2 plates. Layer with fried eggplant and top with prawns. Serve immediately.

* Crème Fraîche: Combine 1 cup (250 mL) whipping cream and 2 tbsp (30 mL) buttermilk in a glass container. Cover; let stand at room temperature for 8 to 24 hours, or until very thick. Stir well before covering; refrigerate up to 10 days.

** This hot chili is actually a dried, smoked jalapeño. It has a wrinkled, dark brown skin and a smoky, sweet, almost chocolatey flavor. Chipotles can be found dried, pickled and canned.

● ● ○ ○

SERVES 2

Recipe courtesy of Urban Ojas Restaurant
    and Juice Bar

Photography: Brian Gould

Pair With:
• Bonterra Cabernet Sauvignon

(G)rilled Thai Prawns Skewered with Lemon Grass

1 tbsp (15 mL) brown sugar
2 tbsp (30 mL) peanut oil
4 garlic cloves, finely minced
1" (2.5 cm) piece of ginger, peeled and finely chopped
1 Thai chili, seeded and finely chopped
juice of 2 limes
1/4 cup (60 mL) rice vinegar
2 tbsp (30 mL) sweet chili sauce
1/4 cup (60 mL) ponzu*
2 tbsp (30 mL) ketchup
30 jumbo size black tiger prawns, peeled and deveined
6 lemon grass stalks, outer skins removed
kosher salt and white pepper to taste
black and white toasted sesame seeds

• • • •

Combine all ingredients in a glass bowl, except shrimp, lemon grass, salt, pepper and sesame seeds. Mix well; add shrimp and stir to combine. Refrigerate for 1 hour.

Trim each piece of lemon grass to a diameter of about 1/4" (6 mm). Using a knife, cut a sharp point on one end of each lemon grass stalk. Preheat a gas grill. Skewer 3 to 5 shrimp through both the head and tail with each lemon grass stalk. Season with salt and pepper. Grill for about 5 minutes per side. Remove from heat and dust with sesame seeds; serve immediately.

* **Ponzu:** citrus-seasoned soy sauce available in Asian specialty stores

• • • •

SERVES 4 TO 6

Recipe by Brandon Boone
Photography: Brian Gould

Pair With:
• German Riesling
• Alsatian Pinot Gris
• B.C. Gewürztraminer

Can Can Crab Legs with Drawn Butter

1/2 cup (125 mL) butter
1 garlic clove, mashed
8 king crab legs
frisee lettuce OR curly endive

● ● ○ ○

Preheat oven to 400°F (200°C).

In a skillet over low heat, melt butter; add garlic and simmer for 5 minutes. Skim milk solids from top of butter and strain out garlic.

Bake crab legs until hot, approximately 10 to 12 minutes. Arrange crab legs like a dancer's legs on a plate. Make a skirt out of lettuce. Drizzle plate with butter and serve remaining butter on the side.

● ● ○ ○

SERVES 4

Recipe by chef Alex Svenne
Photography: Brian Gould

Pair With:
• California Chardonnay
• Chablis
• Australian Viognier

Rainbow Trout with Wasabi Lime Butter, Basmati Rice & Seasonal Vegetables

Wasabi Lime Butter:
1 tbsp (15 mL) ready-made wasabi
1/2 cup (125 mL) unsalted butter
grated zest of 1 lime

Basmati Rice:
1 tbsp (15 mL) butter, for frying
1 small onion, diced
1 cup (250 mL) basmati rice
2 cups (500 mL) vegetable stock

8 asparagus spears
1/4 roasted red pepper, peeled, seeded
1 kale leaf, coarsely chopped
4, 5 oz (140 g) rainbow trout fillets
salt and pepper, to taste
canola oil for frying

● ● ○ ○

Butter: Place all ingredients in a bowl, beat with an electric mixer until smooth.

Rice: In a saucepan, melt butter; add onion and sweat until translucent. Add rice and cook, stirring, for 1 to 2 minutes. Add stock and bring to a boil. Cover and simmer for approximately 20 minutes, or until rice is cooked through.

Steam asparagus for 5 to 6 minutes. Add red pepper and kale and heat through.

Season trout fillets on both sides. In a hot pan; sear fillets skin-side down. Flip fillets and cook until cooked through, 3 to 4 minutes.

● ● ○ ○

SERVES 4

Recipe courtesy of Urban Ojas Restaurant and Juice Bar
Photography: Brian Gould

Pair With:
• Bonterra Chardonnay

ainted Fish

3 limes
2 jalapeño peppers, thinly sliced
1 cup (250 mL) minced fresh cilantro
2 tbsp (30 mL) butter
coarse salt and freshly ground pepper
2 lbs (1 kg) northern pike fillets OR other firm white fish
1 cup (250 g) sliced fresh brown mushrooms
2 Roma tomatoes, sliced
1 medium purple onion, thinly sliced

● ● ● ●

Squeeze 2 limes into a small food processor. Add 1 jalapeño pepper and the cilantro. Pulse until a thick paste forms. Add more lime juice if necessary.

On a large sheet of heavy-duty aluminum foil, spread 1 tbsp (15 mL) butter. Sprinkle with salt and pepper. Place 1 lb (450 g) of fish on foil. Paint fish with cilantro-lime mixture. Top with mushrooms, tomatoes and onion. Fold foil to make a tight packet. Repeat with the remaining fish.

Place packets on medium-hot area of fire pit grill for 12 to 15 minutes. Remove from fire. Open packet carefully. Drain off juices. Garnish with jalapeño and cilantro.

● ● ● ●

SERVES 4-6

Recipe by Shel Zolkewich
Photography: Brian Gould

Pistachio-Crusted Catfish
with Orange Chipotle Cream Sauce

Pistachios:
2 cups (500 mL) shelled, lightly toasted pistachios
1 tsp (5 mL) minced garlic
1 tbsp (15 mL) Asiago OR Parmesan cheese
1 tsp (5 mL) kosher salt
1 tsp (5 mL) white pepper
1 tbsp (15 mL) chopped parsley
1/2 cup (125 mL) bread crumbs

Catfish:
8, 6 oz (175 g) catfish fillets
flour
1 egg, beaten and mixed with 1 tbsp (15 mL) water

Orange Chipotle Cream Sauce:
1 tbsp (15 mL) butter
1 tbsp (15 mL) canola oil
1 cup (250 mL) diced white onion
1 tbsp (15 mL) minced garlic
1/2 tsp (2 mL) kosher salt
1/2 tbsp (7.5 mL) white pepper
2 minced chipotle peppers
1 tbsp (15 mL) chipotle sauce
3 cups (750 mL) vegetable OR seafood stock
grated zest of 2 oranges
1/2 cup (125 mL) orange juice
1/2 cup (125 mL) flour
1/2 cup (125 mL) whipping cream

● ● ● ●

Pistachios: Process all ingredients together to make fine crumbs.

Catfish: Coat catfish with flour, then dip in eggwash; coat with pistachio crumbs. Set aside.

Sauce: Heat butter and oil in a skillet over medium heat; add onion and garlic. Sauté until onion is translucent. Add salt, pepper, peppers and sauce; cook for 5 minutes, stirring occasionally. Add stock, zest and orange juice. Bring to a boil, reduce heat and simmer for 5 minutes. Strain sauce through a sieve, using the back of a ladle to push out all the liquid.

istachio-Crusted Catfish

(continued)

Return sauce to skillet and bring to a boil. Mix flour and water together; stir 3/4 cup (175 mL) of sauce into flour mixture to temper. Stir flour mixture into sauce; reduce heat and simmer for 5 to 10 minutes, or until thickened.

Pan-sear catfish in oil over medium-high heat and finish in a 350°F (180°C) oven for 5 to 8 minutes. Drizzle sauce over catfish while hot.

● ● ○ ○

SERVES 4

Recipe by chef Darcy Fry

Photography: Hamid Attie Photography

Pair With:
- Côtes du Rhône White
- California Chardonnay
- B.C. Meritage

(S)eared Albacore Tuna with Syrah Sauce

Syrah Sauce:
3/4 cup (175 mL) Syrah wine
  OR any other full-bodied
  wine
2 oranges segmented, with
  any juice reserved
2 shallots
bouquet of herbs (such as
  parsley, oregano, thyme)
1/4 cup (60 mL) fish fumet*
1/4 cup (60 mL) cold butter
6 black olives, pitted
6 green olives, pitted
6 peeled cherry tomatoes

olive oil for dressing and for
  cooking
8 oz (250 g) sashimi-grade
  albacore tuna, cut into
  6 equal medallions
salt and pepper to taste
6 small sprigs of rosemary
6 scallions
spring peas sautéed with
  double-smoked bacon and
  reserved on a warm plate

● ● ● ●

Sauce: In a saucepan over medium-high heat, combine wine, orange juice, shallots and herb bouquet; bring to a boil then reduce heat to a simmer. Let reduce by half; add fumet and let reduce by half. Remove herbs and whisk in cold butter. Once incorporated, add orange segments, olives and tomatoes. Keep sauce warm until ready to use.

Heat oil in a nonstick skillet over medium-high heat. Season tuna medallions on both sides with salt and pepper. Sear tuna with the rosemary sprigs and scallions.

Divide sautéed spring peas with bacon among 6 plates. Place 1 tuna medallion on top, adding 1 rosemary sprig and 1 scallion for each plate. Drizzle tuna with Syrah Sauce and serve immediately.

* a concentrated fish stock

● ● ● ●

SERVES 6

Recipe by chef Guiseppe Posteraro
Photography: Hamid Attie Photography

Pair With:
• Italian Valpolicella
• Oregon Pinot Noir
• Côtes du Rhone Villages

Pepito Crusted Tuna Steak with Chipotle Lime Sauce

Chipotle Lime Sauce:
1 tsp (5 mL) puréed chipotle
   peppers in adobe sauce*
grated zest of 1 lime
juice of half a lime
1/4 cup (60 mL) mayonnaise
1/4 cup (60 mL) yogurt OR sour
   cream

1/2 cup (125 mL) pumpkin seeds
   (pepitos), extra for garnish
1 tbsp (15 mL) cumin seed
1 tbsp (15 mL) kosher OR coarse
   sea salt
1 tbsp (15 mL) cracked black
   pepper
1 tsp (5 mL) dried chile flakes
2 lb (1 kg) tuna steak
1 tbsp (15 mL) canola oil
juice from half a lime

Sauce: Combine all sauce ingredients and mix well. Set aside.

Toast pumpkin and cumin seeds in a 350°F (180°C) oven for 5 minutes. In a food processor or coffee grinder, grind pumpkin and cumin to a coarse meal.

Combine pumpkin seeds and cumin with salt, pepper and chiles. Crust tuna steak with pumpkin seed mixture.

Brush a heavy skillet with canola oil and heat. Sear tuna steak over medium-high heat for about 2 minutes. The bottom should be white around the edges. Flip tuna over and sear for 1 minute. Drizzle with lime juice; cover steak and remove from heat. Let sit 5 minutes. Steak should still be very rare. With a very sharp knife, slice tuna steak on an angle in thin slices. Arrange slices on a platter and drizzle with sauce. Garnish with lime wedges, toasted pumpkin seeds and sprigs of cilantro.

* Available at specialty stores or use 1/2 tsp (2 mL) dried ground chipotle pepper. In a pinch, substitute chili powder.

SERVES 4

Recipe by chef Alex Svenne
Photography: Brian Gould

Pair With:
• Ravenswood Zinfandel

Grilled Salmon Steaks with Sorrel-Spinach Sauce

Sorrel-Spinach Sauce:
2 shallots
1 tsp (5 mL) unsalted butter
1/2 cup (125 mL) dry white wine
1 bunch spinach, washed, stems discarded
1 bunch sorrel* leaves, washed, stems discarded
1 lemon, zest only
1/2 tsp (2.5 mL) cracked fennel seeds
2 tbsp (30 mL) minced fresh herbs such as thyme, tarragon OR lemon thyme
2 green onions, minced
1/2 cup (125 mL) buttermilk
kosher salt and hot chile flakes, to taste

4, 6 oz (175 g) salmon steaks
salt and pepper, to taste
canola oil

• • • •

Sauce: In a skillet, melt butter and sauté shallots, without browning, until tender. Add wine, bring to a boil and add spinach, turning leaves with tongs until just wilted. Purée in a food processor with the sorrel leaves. Add remaining ingredients, thinning to desired consistency with buttermilk. Season with salt and pepper to taste.

Preheat a gas grill or charcoal barbecue. Season salmon with salt and pepper; brush with a little canola oil. Place on grill and cook 4 to 6 minutes a side, or until cooked. Place a dollop of sauce on each salmon steak and serve immediately.

* **Sorrel:** This irrepressible perennial tastes of tart young green apple and makes a lovely refreshing summer partner for grilled salmon, shrimp and other high-fat fish.

• • • •

SERVES 4

Recipe by dee Hobsbawn-Smith

Photography: Brian Gould

Pair With:
• B.C. Pinot Blanc
• Burgundy Aligoté
• Rioja Rosé

Seared Scotch Salmon

4, 6 oz (175 g) salmon fillets
salt and pepper, to taste
3 garlic cloves, finely minced
2 tbsp (30 mL) minced fresh parsley
1/4 cup (60 mL) olive oil, divided
8 oz (250 g) brown mushrooms
1/4 cup (60 mL) sweet chile sauce
1/4 cup (60 mL) single malt Scotch whisky (such as Glenfiddich)
2 tsp (10 mL) grated orange zest
20 mandarin orange wedges

● ● ○ ●

Season salmon with salt and pepper. Combine garlic, parsley and 1 tbsp (15 ml) oil; rub salmon with mixture. Heat remaining oil in a skillet over medium-high heat. Add salmon and sear for 3 to 4 minutes a side, or until fish flakes easily. Remove from pan and keep warm. Add mushrooms to pan and sauté until browned. Add remaining ingredients to pan and continue to cook until slightly reduced.

Spoon sauce over reserved salmon and garnish with additional mandarin wedges.

● ● ○ ●

SERVES: 4

Recipe by Brandon Boone
Photography: Brian Gould

Herb-Crusted Braided Salmon

Lemon-Cream Sauce:
1/2 cup (125 mL) whipping cream
1/2 cup (125 mL) mayonnaise
finely grated zest of 1 lemon
pinch of salt

Herb-Crusted Braided Salmon:
3 lb (1.2 kg) boneless, skinless salmon fillet
extra-virgin olive oil for brushing
Dijon mustard for brushing
salt and freshly ground pepper
3 tbsp (45 mL) EACH, chopped fresh tarragon, parsley and chives

● ● ● ●

Sauce: In a chilled metal bowl, whip cream until stiff peaks form. Beat in mayonnaise. Fold in zest and salt. Refrigerate 20 minutes to allow flavours to develop.

Salmon: Preheat oven to 400°F (200°C). Wash salmon and pat dry. Lay fillet on a flat surface with inside facing up and wide end closest to you. With a sharp knife or pizza cutter, cut fillet lengthwise into 3 equal strips, leaving 1" (2.5 cm) of the tail end intact. Brush with oil and mustard. Sprinkle with salt, freshly ground pepper and chopped herbs.

Press seasonings onto salmon with fingers. Braid salmon, securing wide end with a wooden skewer. Tuck narrow end under. Place braided fillet on a parchment paper-lined rimmed baking sheet. Bake at for 25 to 28 minutes. Remove to a serving platter and serve with Lemon Cream Sauce.

● ● ● ●

SERVES 4

Recipe by CJ Katz
Photography: Brian Gould

Grilled Halibut with Walnut & Coriander Sauce

Based loosely on muhammara, a classic Turkish relish, this sauce has migrated throughout the Middle East as a garnish for several grilled ingredients such as bread, fish and meats, or as a resplendent star appetizer.

Walnut & Coriander Sauce:
1/4 lb (125 g) walnut halves
1/4 cup (60 mL) diced tomato
1/4 cup (60 mL) pomegranate
  molasses
1 tsp (5 mL) toasted ground
  cumin
1 tbsp (15 mL) honey
1/2 tsp (2.5 mL) sumac
juice of 1 lemon
1 garlic clove, minced
2 tbsp (30 mL) extra-virgin
  olive oil
2 tbsp (30 mL) walnut oil
2 tbsp (30 mL) minced cilantro
salt and hot chile flakes, to
  taste
4, 6 oz (175 g) halibut steaks
olive oil

● ● ○ ●

Preheat oven to 350°F (180°C).

Sauce: Place walnuts on a baking sheet in a single layer and toast them for 10 to 15 minutes. Remove from the oven and cool thoroughly, then chop with a knife. Set aside. Whisk together tomato and pomegranate molasses; stir in cumin, honey, sumac, lemon juice and garlic. Add oils, whisking well. Stir in cilantro. Add salt, hot chile flakes and walnuts.

Preheat a gas grill or charcoal barbecue. Season halibut with salt and pepper and brush with oil. Place steaks on grill and cook 6 to 8 minutes a side, or until cooked. Remove halibut from heat and brush with sauce.

● ● ○ ●

SERVES 4

Recipe by dee Hobsbawn-Smith
Photography: Brian Gould

Pair With:
• California Chardonnay
• Fino Sherry
• Loire Valley Chenin Blanc

Thyme & Lemon Pepper Crusted Halibut with Ratatouille

Ratatouille:
3 tbsp (45 mL) olive oil
7 oz (205 g) white
  mushrooms, sliced
1 small eggplant, peeled and
  diced
1 medium zucchini squash,
  peeled and diced
1 red bell pepper, diced
1 small onion, diced
2 tomatoes, peeled, seeded
  and diced
4 fresh basil leaves, julienned
1 tsp (5 mL) chopped fresh
  oregano
2 garlic cloves, minced
salt and pepper, to taste

Halibut:
4, 6 oz (175 g) halibut fillets
salt and pepper, to taste
1 tbsp (15 mL) olive oil
1 tbsp (15 mL) finely chopped
  fresh thyme (remove stems)
1 tbsp (15 mL) minced lemon
  zest
1 tsp (5 mL) freshly cracked
  black pepper

● ● ○ ○ ○

Ratatouille: Heat oil in a skillet over medium-high heat. When hot, add mushrooms, eggplant, zucchini, red pepper, onion, tomatoes and sauté. Let simmer for a few minutes. Add basil, oregano, garlic, salt and pepper and simmer for 1 minute.

Halibut: Preheat oven to 350°F (180°C). Season halibut lightly with salt and pepper. Heat oil in a skillet over medium-high heat. Add halibut and sear until golden brown on each side. Place on a heatproof platter. Combine thyme, lemon zest and cracked pepper; coat top of halibut. Bake halibut for 8 to 10 minutes.

Place ratatouille on a warmed plate; top with halibut, crust side up. Serve immediately.

● ● ○ ○ ○

SERVES 4

Recipe by chef Albertino Costa

Photography: Brian Gould

Pair With:
● Washington State
  Sauvignon Blanc
● Loire Valley White
● B.C. Pinot Gris

Halibut Steaks Baked in Sauvignon Blanc & Mustard Fennel Butter

Mustard Fennel Butter:
2 tsp (10 mL) fennel seeds, toasted and ground
1 tsp (5 mL) coriander seeds, toasted and ground
1/3 cup (75 mL) salted butter, at room temperature
1/4 cup (60 mL) chopped fresh parsley
1 chipotle pepper in adobo sauce, minced
3 tbsp (45 mL) Dijon mustard
salt and pepper, to taste

4, 6 oz (175 g) halibut steaks
1 cup (250 mL) Sauvignon Blanc

● ● ◦ ◦

Butter: Combine fennel, coriander, butter, parsley, chipotle pepper and mustard in a small bowl. Mash together, using a spatula, until smooth and well blended. Season butter mixture with salt and pepper to taste; reserve butter mixture at room temperature.

Preheat oven to 375°F (190°C).

Sprinkle halibut with salt and pepper. Place in an 8" (20 cm) square glass baking dish. Pour wine over halibut. Bake until opaque in centre, basting occasionally with wine and juices in dish, for approximately 15 minutes, or until fish flakes easily. Divide fish among 4 plates. Spread all of the Mustard Fennel Butter over fish.

● ● ◦ ◦

SERVES 4

Recipe by Brandon Boone
Photography: Brian Gould

Pair With:
• New Zealand Sauvignon Blanc
• White Bordeaux
• Sancerre

Cherry Tomato, Bay Leaf & Lemon Chicken Skewers

Bay leaves are from the evergreen bay laurel tree, native to the Mediterranean. Early Greeks and Romans thought the aromatic leaves had magical properties. A staple in soups and stews, this herb can turn grilled skewers into something spectacular. The heat from the barbecue releases the oils in the fresh leaves and infuses foods with fabulous flavour.

Lemon Herb Marinade:
grated zest and juice of 1 lemon
1/4 cup (60 mL) olive oil
1 tbsp (15 mL) minced fresh oregano
1 tbsp (15 mL) minced fresh rosemary
4 garlic cloves, minced
1 tsp (5 mL) kosher salt
1 tsp (5 mL) freshly cracked pepper

4 chicken breasts, cut into 1/2" (1.3 cm) cubes
1 pkg fresh bay leaves*, washed and cut in half
1 container cherry tomatoes
1 zucchini, cut into chunks
1 yellow sweet bell pepper, cored, seeded and cut into chunks
12" (30 cm) bamboo skewers

● ● ● ○

Marinade: In a bowl, whisk together lemon zest, juice, oil, herbs, garlic, salt and pepper. Remove 1 tbsp (15 mL) of marinade and reserve.

Combine chicken and marinade. Turn to coat; cover and refrigerate for 30 minutes, stirring every 10 minutes. Remove chicken from marinade and thread on bamboo skewers, alternating with bay leaf, tomato, zucchini and pepper; repeat until all ingredients are used. Grill skewers on a preheated barbecue until chicken is cooked. Just before serving, brush with reserved marinade.

* You can find fresh bay leaves in the herb section of some supermarkets or try growing your own at home. You can use dry leaves but they have a fraction of the flavour.

● ● ● ○

Recipe by Brandon Boone
Photography: Brian Gould

innamon-Skewered Chicken with Plums & Peppers

4 boneless, skinless chicken breasts
salt and pepper, to taste
4, 5–6" (13–15 cm) cinnamon sticks
2 ripe plums
1 red bell pepper, cored, seeded and cut into 1" (2.5 cm) pieces
1 green bell pepper, cored, seeded and cut into 1" (2.5 cm) pieces

● ● ● ○

Season chicken breasts with salt and pepper then cut into 3/4" (2 cm) cubes. Cut plums in half down the crease. Twist halves in opposite direction to separate. Remove pit. Cut plum halves into 2 wedges each, then in half vertically to make 1" (2.5 cm) square chunks. Using a bamboo skewer or knife, poke a hole through the centres of chicken, plums and peppers.

Preheat a gas barbecue to medium-low. Thread ingredients alternately onto cinnamon sticks. Place skewers on barbecue. Grill 2 minutes each side, flip and repeat until chicken is cooked through. Remove from heat; tent and let sit for 3 minutes. Uncover and serve immediately.

● ● ● ○

Recipe by Brandon Boone

Photography: Brian Gould

Pair With:
• B.C. Merlot
• Red Costières de Nimes
• Oregon Pinot Noir

Grilled Half Chicken with Raspberry Mustard Barbecue Sauce

Raspberry Mustard
  Barbecue Sauce:
2 tbsp (30 mL) butter
1/4 cup (60 mL) minced sweet
  onion
1 tbsp (15 mL) minced garlic
1 tbsp (15 mL) minced red New
  Mexico chile
1/2 cup (125 mL) raspberries, fresh
  or frozen (unsweetened)
1 cup (250 mL) raspberry ale
  (e.g.: Mort Subite Framboise, Wild
  Rose Wraspberry Ale)
1/3 cup (75 mL) Dijon mustard
1 tbsp (15 mL) brown sugar
1/4 tsp (1 mL) salt
1/2 tsp (2 mL) pink peppercorns

3 lb (1.5 kg) whole chicken, backbone removed and cut in half
salt and pepper, to taste

● ● ● ●

Sauce: Melt butter in large, heavy skillet over low heat. Cook onion and garlic, stirring occasionally, until garlic is tender, about 2 minutes. Add remaining ingredients and simmer 15 minutes.

Place raspberry mixture in a blender and purée on high. Press purée through a sieve for a perfectly smooth sauce.

Preheat a barbecue to medium. Season each side of chicken with salt and pepper. Place chicken on grill, skin side down. Reduce heat to medium low. Turn chicken 45 degrees after 5 to 7 minutes. Flip over and repeat. Continue to grill until chicken is fully cooked, or until juices run clear when pierced with a toothpick. Brush with sauce and cook for an additional 5 minutes. Remove from heat and cover with aluminum foil for 5 minutes. Uncover and serve.

● ● ● ●

SERVES 2 – MAKES ABOUT 1 1/2 CUPS (375 ML) OF SAUCE

Recipe by Lucy Saunders
Photography: Brian Gould

Barbecued Chicken Legs with Mango Sauce

I love this sauce for its simplicity – no fat, oodles of flavour and a colour that would have had van Gogh drooling.

Mango Sauce:
2 very ripe mangoes, peeled and pitted
1/2 cup (125 mL) orange juice
grated zest of 1 orange
1 tbsp (15 mL) grated fresh ginger root
1 tsp (5 mL) sherry vinegar
1 tbsp (15 mL) melted honey
1 tbsp (15 mL) minced red bell pepper
1 tbsp (15 mL) minced dried cranberries OR cherries (optional)
1/2 apple, sliced into matchsticks (optional)
hot chile flakes, to taste
kosher salt, to taste
2 tbsp (30 mL) minced fresh herbs such as thyme, parsley, Thai basil OR cilantro

10 chicken legs
salt and pepper, to taste

● ● ● ●

Sauce: Purée mango pulp, add remaining sauce ingredients to purée, thinning with additional orange juice if needed. Season with salt and pepper to taste.

Preheat a gas grill or charcoal barbecue to low. Season chicken with salt and pepper. Place chicken on grill and cook for 15 to 20 minutes, turning every 5 minutes, or until cooked. Remove from heat and brush with Mango Sauce before serving.

● ● ● ●

SERVES 4

Recipe by dee Hobsbawn-Smith
Photography: Brian Gould

Pair With:
● India Pale Ale
● Verdicchio
● New Zealand Chardonnay

(J)erk Chicken

The spirit of jerk barbecuing is similar to an island vacation, informal and all about going with the flow. Experiment with your own spice and sauce concoctions, as JamRock's Don Woodstock isn't giving away the secret to his signature blend.

4 5 chicken pieces
3 cups (750 mL) cane vinegar
JamRock all-purpose
　　seasoning OR your own jerk
　　blend*
JamRock jerk sauce**

● ● ● ○

Rinse chicken in cane vinegar and pat dry. Season well with jerk seasoning, including beneath skin. Brush jerk sauce over chicken to coat. Seal chicken pieces in a large resealable plastic bag, squeezing out any air before closing. Refrigerate for a minimum of 2 hours.

Preheat oven to 350°F (180°C). Bake chicken for 45 minutes, turning pieces once midway through cooking time. Alternately, place chicken skin-side down on a well-oiled barbecue grill preheated to low. Close the lid. Once the skin is golden brown and crispy, turn chicken over and cook until internal temperature reaches 170°F (77°C).

* Jerk Seasoning: Start with a combination of 1 Scotch bonnet pepper, seeded and minced (leave the seeds if you want a fiery jerk. Protect your hands with gloves while chopping pepper), 2 tbsp (30 mL) allspice, 1 tbsp (15 mL) thyme, 1 tsp (5 mL) each salt and black pepper and 1/4 tsp (1 mL) each cinnamon and nutmeg.

** Jerk Sauce: Combine jerk seasoning with 2 tbsp (30 mL) soy sauce, 1/4 cup (60 mL) vegetable oil, 1/2 cup (125 mL) lime, orange or pineapple juice, rum (to taste), 2 to 3 crushed garlic cloves and 2 finely sliced green onions.

Note: The jerk seasoning and sauce work equally well with pork. If preparing pork chops for the oven or grill, there is no need to rinse with the cane vinegar. Pork on the grill should reach an internal temperature of 160°F (71°C).

● ● ● ○

Recipe by Don Woodstock

Photography: Brian Gould

Pair With:
• Loire Valley Chenin Blanc
• Australian Sauvignon Blanc
• India Pale Ale

Island Boucanier Chicken

This marinade can be used for meats, fish and poultry.

Garlic, Lime and Rum Marinade:
1 tbsp (15 mL) salt
1 tsp (5 mL) grated nutmeg
1 tsp (5 mL) grated fresh ginger
2 tbsp (30 mL) chopped fresh thyme
1 tsp (5 mL) paprika
1 tsp (5 mL) cayenne
4 garlic cloves, finely chopped
2 tbsp (30 mL) fresh lime juice OR lemon juice
2 oz (60 mL) West Indian Rum
1 tbsp (15 mL) West Indian cane sugar
1 Scotch bonnet pepper, finely chopped (optional)

1 whole chicken, cut into parts

● ● ● ○

Marinade: Combine all ingredients in a bowl.

Baste chicken thoroughly with marinade, reserving excess. Cover chicken and refrigerate for 2 to 3 hours. Preheat a gas barbecue to medium. Grill chicken, basting continually with reserved marinade, for 25 to 30 minutes, turning occasionally.

● ● ● ○

SERVES 4 TO 6

Recipe by Rookmin Maharaj
Photography: John Ulan/Epic Photography

Pair With:
• Amber Ale
• B.C. Gewürztraminer
• Ontario Riesling

Seared Chicken Breasts with Spicy Pancetta, Rosemary & Chardonnay

2 tbsp (30 mL) olive oil
2 whole chickens, cut into legs, thighs and breasts
salt and pepper, to taste
8 oz (250 g) thick-cut spicy pancetta, chopped
7 garlic cloves, chopped
2 tbsp (30 mL) chopped fresh rosemary
1 1/4 cups (310 mL) Chardonnay
1 cup (250 mL) chicken broth
12 oz (341 mL) can chopped tomatoes
1 tbsp (15 mL) tomato purée
fresh rosemary sprigs for garnish

● ● ● ○

Preheat oven to 375°F (190°C).

Heat oil in a large ovenproof pot over medium-high heat. Season chicken with salt and pepper. Working in batches, sauté chicken until golden, approximately 4 minutes per side. Remove chicken from pot and add pancetta, garlic and rosemary; sauté for 1 minute. Add Chardonnay, chicken broth, and tomatoes. Bring to boil, scraping up browned bits, and cook for 5 minutes.

Return chicken to pot and cover; place in oven. Bake until chicken breasts are cooked through, approximately 15 minutes. Remove chicken breasts from pot and continue baking until drumsticks and thighs are cooked through, approximately 10 minutes longer. Remove pot from oven and transfer chicken to a platter; tent with foil.

Place pot over medium-high heat and boil liquids until reduced to 2 cups (500 mL). Season sauce with salt and pepper. Pour sauce over chicken. Garnish with rosemary sprigs and serve.

● ● ● ○

SERVES 6

Recipe by Brandon Boone
Photography: Brian Gould

Pair With:
• White Burgundy
• Italian Chardonnay
• California Marsanne

sian-Brined Chicken with Peanut Sauce

Asian Brine:
1 recipe basic brine (page 181)
1 cup (250 mL) dark soy sauce
2 oranges, squeezed into brine and tossed in
1 tsp (5 mL) dried chile flakes
1/4 cup (60 mL) coarsely chopped ginger
1/4 cup (60 mL) coarsely chopped garlic
1 whole chicken OR duck

Peanut Sauce:
1/4 cup (60 mL) sesame oil
1 tbsp (15 mL) minced garlic
1 tbsp (15 mL) minced ginger
1 tsp (5 mL) chile flakes, or more to taste
1/2 cup (125 mL) peanut butter
1 tbsp (15 mL) soy sauce
1/2 cup (125 mL) water
1/2 cup (125 mL) chopped green onions

● ● ● ○

Brine: Combine all ingredients in a large pot. Cover and refrigerate for 24 hours or up to 3 days. Remove chicken from brine and rinse. Remove backbone and butterfly chicken.

Sauce: Heat oil in a skillet over medium-high heat; sauté garlic, ginger and chile flakes. Add remaining ingredients, except green onion. Bring to a low boil and stir well. Stir in green onion. Remove from heat and cover until ready to use.

Prepare a gas or charcoal barbecue for offset cooking. Place chicken on grill and cook with offset heat for 45 minutes, turning over at the halfway point. Brush liberally with sauce and cook for an additional 3 minutes. Remove from heat; let stand for 5 minutes before carving.

Thai Brine: Add 1 can coconut milk, 1/4 cup (60 mL) chopped Thai basil, 1/4 cup (60 mL) chopped mint and 1/4 cup (60 mL) chopped cilantro. Substitute a lime for the orange.

● ● ● ○

SERVES 4

Recipe by chef Alex Svenne
Photography: Brian Gould

Pair With:
• Oregon Pinot Gris
• Australian Semillon
• Alsatian Pinto Blanc

astels

Ginger Garlic Chicken Filling:
1 tsp (5 mL) paprika
1 tsp (5 mL) granulated garlic
1 tsp (5 mL) ground ginger
1/4 tsp (1 mL) salt
1 Scotch bonnet pepper, minced (optional)
1 tbsp (15 mL) chopped cilantro
2 chicken breasts, cut into small pieces OR 1lb (500 g) ground chicken
1 tbsp (15 mL) canola OR corn oil
1 tbsp (15 mL) brown cane sugar
2 medium tomatoes, diced
1 onion, diced

Masa Harina Dough:
3 cups (750 mL) masa harina (corn flour)
2 tbsp (30 mL) butter
1 pinch of salt
2 cups (500 mL) water

6 to 8 banana leaves (found in the freezer aisle of most supermarkets)
3 cups (750 mL) water
twine

● ● ● ○

Filling: Mix first 6 ingredients together; add chicken and marinate for at least 2 hours. Heat oil in a skillet over medium heat; add sugar. Stir until sugar is frothy and golden brown. Add chicken. Cook at high heat for 3 to 5 minutes, stirring frequently. Reduce heat to medium. Add tomatoes and onion; cover and simmer for at least 15 minutes. Let cool to room temperature.

Dough: Combine all ingredients in a bowl and mix well. Dough should be soft and pasty to the touch. Let dough rest for 10 minutes. Add additional water if dough is too dry. Set aside.

Wash banana leaves thoroughly before use. Cut banana leaves in rectangles of 6 x 12" (15 x 30 cm). If banana leaves break, patch with additional leaves.

Pastels
(continued)

Place 2 tbsp (30 mL) of dough in the centre of a banana rectangle. Use bottom of a spoon to flatten and spread dough to 6" (15 cm) in diameter. Place 2 tbsp (30 mL) of filling on dough. Take another 2 tbsp (30 mL) of dough and flatten in hands to form a 4" (10 cm) round. Place on top of filling, pressing lightly to seal. Fold one end of banana leaf and cover dough. Continue folding the other 3 sides, forming a rectangular parcel (about 3 x 5"/8 x 13 cm). Tie securely with twine. Repeat for desired number of parcels. Fill a large pot with water and bring to a boil. Place parcels in the water. Cook for at least 10 minutes. Remove from water with a slotted spoon. Untie parcels and serve. Parcels may be served as a side dish or as an entrée.

● ● ● ○

SERVES 4 TO 6

Recipe by Rookmin Maharaj

Photography: John Ulan/Epic Photography

Pair With:
- Mexican Pilsner
- India Pale Ale
- B.C. Riesling

ⓟ an-Seared Chicken Breast with Chive & Garlic Smashed Potatoes & Roasted Tomato Broth

Roasted Tomatoes:
1 tbsp (15 mL) EACH, chopped fresh thyme, rosemary, parsley and basil
1/4 cup (60 mL) olive oil
10 Roma tomatoes, quartered lengthwise
3 garlic cloves, minced
kosher salt and freshly ground pepper

Pan-Seared Chicken:
6 skin-on, bone-in chicken breasts
salt and pepper, to taste
Montreal steak spice
2 tbsp (30 mL) olive oil
parchment paper

Olive Broth:
1/4 cup (60 mL) olive oil
1 tbsp (15 mL) minced garlic
1 1/2 cups (375 mL) chopped fresh fennel
2 cups (500 mL) diced purple onion
1/2 cup (125 mL) white wine
3 cups (750 mL) chicken stock
1 cup (250 mL) packed spinach chiffonade (thin strips or shreds)
1 cup (250 mL) chopped kalamata olives
kosher salt and freshly ground pepper

Chive & Garlic Smashed Potatoes:
6 Yukon Gold potatoes, peeled and diced
1/2 cup (125 mL) olive oil
1 onion, finely diced
1 tbsp (15 mL) puréed roasted garlic
1 cup (250 mL) chicken stock
salt and pepper, to taste
2 tbsp (30 mL) thinly sliced chives

● ● ● ●

Tomatoes: Preheat oven to 350°F (180°C). Put herbs, oil and garlic in a large bowl. Add tomatoes and toss several times to coat; season with salt and pepper. Spread tomatoes on a parchment-lined pan and roast for at least 1 hour, turning halfway. If still quite firm, cook up to 15 minutes longer.

Chicken: Preheat oven to 350°F (180°C). Season chicken breasts with salt, pepper and Montreal steak spice. In a large sauté pan, heat oil over medium-high heat until almost smoking. Carefully add chicken to pan skin side down. Sear until very golden brown, about 5 minutes. Turn chicken over and cook other side until golden brown. Remove from pan and place on a parchment-lined baking sheet. Place in oven and cook 20 to 30 minutes, or until juices run clear when pierced with a knife.

Pan-Seared Chicken Breast with Chive & Garlic Smashed Potatoes & Roasted Tomato Broth

(continued)

Broth: Over medium heat, pour oil into the same sauté pan in which the chicken was cooked. Add garlic, fennel and onion to pan and sauté 5 minutes. Deglaze with white wine. Slowly add chicken stock; bring to a boil and reduce sauce to approximately 3 cups (750 mL), about 15 minutes Add spinach and olives; cook another 2 minutes. Season broth with salt and pepper. Add cooked chicken to sauté pan and turn to coat in broth. Cover and reduce heat until ready to serve.

Potatoes: In a medium saucepan, bring water to a boil. Add potatoes and salt; cook until very tender. While potatoes are cooking, heat oil in a heavy-bottomed pan over low heat; add onions and sauté until caramelized, approximately 20 minutes. Drain potatoes and mash with potato masher. Add roasted garlic purée, onions and 1/2 cup (125 mL) chicken stock. Using an electric mixer, whip potatoes on high speed, turn to low and add remaining chicken stock (use less or more stock depending on desired consistency). Season generously with salt and pepper. Stir in chives.

Divide potatoes among 6 large, shallow pasta bowls. Top with roasted tomatoes and the chicken, skin side up. Ladle sauce around potatoes. Garnish with a fresh sprig of rosemary or thyme.

● ● ● ○

SERVES 6

Recipe by chef Shelley Martin

Photography: Brian Gould

Sweet Cardamom Chicken

25 cardamom pods, seeds removed and crushed
1" (2.5 cm) fresh ginger, grated
4 garlic cloves, crushed
1 tsp (5 mL) kosher salt
1 tsp (5 mL) pepper
grated zest of 1 lemon
3 lbs (1.5 kg) chicken thighs and legs, skin removed
14 oz (398 mL) coconut milk
1 1/2 cups (375 mL) chicken stock
3 jalapeños, sliced
1 onion, diced
2/3 cup (150 mL) yogurt
1 lb (500 g) whole green beans, trimmed
1 lemon, cut into 8 wedges
2 tbsp (30 mL) chopped cilantro leaves

● ● ● ○

Mix cardamom, ginger, garlic, salt, pepper and lemon zest to make a paste; spread over chicken pieces; let rest for 20 minutes. Place chicken, coconut milk, chicken stock, jalapeños and onion in a slow cooker. Cover and cook on low heat for 4 to 5 hours, or until juice from thickest part of chicken is no longer pink when pricked.

Skim fat from sauce; add yogurt and green beans; cook for approximately 10 minutes, or until beans are tender.

Spoon chicken and beans into 4 bowls; pour 1/4 cup (60 mL) sauce from slow cooker over each. Drizzle with juice from lemon wedges and top with cilantro leaves. Serve immediately.

● ● ● ○

SERVES 4

Recipe by Brandon Boone
Photography: Brian Gould

Pair With:
• South African Sauvignon Blanc
• Ontario Riesling
• Oregon Chardonnay

Roast Partridge in a Pear Purée

On the first day of Christmas my true love gave to me, A Partridge in a Pear Tree ...

2 partridges or quail
4 cups (1 L) buttermilk
salt and pepper, to taste

Pear Purée:
4 pears, quartered and seeded
1/2 cup (125 mL) honey

4 sprigs of sage

• • • •

In a resealable plastic bag, combine partridges and buttermilk. Marinate in refrigerator overnight. Discard buttermilk and pat partridges dry. Sprinkle cavity and outside of bird with salt and pepper.

Pear Purée: Preheat oven to 350°F (180°C). Toss pears in honey and bake until a rich mahogany brown, approximately 30 minutes. Remove from oven. Cut 4 small slices from pear and reserve; purée remaining pears and honey.

Preheat oven to 450°F (230°C).

Roast partridges for 12 to 15 minutes. Remove from heat and tent with foil. Let rest 5 minutes. In the centre of 4 plates, spoon pear purée onto each plate. Arrange 1 leg and 1 breast on purée (don't completely hide purée). Garnish with a slice of pear and a sprig of sage.

• • • •

SERVES 4

Recipe by chef Alex Svenne
Photography: Brian Gould

Pair With:
• White Rhone
• Australian Riesling
• Ontario Chardonnay

Seared Magret de Canard with Saskatoon Berry-Red Wine Reduction

1 bottle (750 mL) red wine, preferably Burgundy OR Cabernet Sauvignon
2 cups (500 mL) demi-glaze OR beef stock
1 1/2 cups (375 mL) saskatoon berries, fresh or frozen
4 tbsp (60 mL) cold unsalted butter, cut into small cubes
2 boneless duck breasts, skin on, about 8–12 oz (250–340 g) each
salt and pepper, to taste
parsley chiffonade (thin shreds)

● ● ● ○

Sauce: In a large stainless steel saucepan bring wine to a boil and reduce to 1 cup (250 mL). Add demi-glaze and continue to reduce until 1 cup (250 mL) remains. Add saskatoon berries. Whisk in butter, 1 cube at a time, until slightly thickened. Set aside.

Preheat oven to 400°F (200°C).

Score skin side of duck breast, every 1/2" (1.3 cm) in cross-hatch design. Season both sides of duck breast. Sear skin side down over medium heat in ovenproof heavy-bottomed skillet. When crisp, turn over and sear. Transfer pan to oven and roast about 5 minutes. Meat should be medium rare.

Remove duck from pan, tent and let rest 3 to 5 minutes. Slice breasts on the diagonal into thin slices. To serve, spread a pool of sauce on plate and centre a fan of sliced breast meat on sauce. Garnish with parsley chiffonade.

● ● ● ○

SERVES 4

Recipe by chef Adam Sperling
Photography: Patricia Holdsworth

Pair with:
• Chateauneuf de Pape
• Tempranillo

Cherry-Smoked Duck with Sour Cherry Sauce

Orange Soy Brine:
4 qts (4 L) water
2 cups (500 mL) soy sauce
2 cups (500 mL) orange juice
1 cup (250 mL) kosher salt
1/2 cup (125 mL) brown sugar
1 tbsp (15 mL) peppercorns

1 whole duck
6 Bradley Cherry Wood bisquettes

Sour Cherry Sauce:
1 tsp (5 mL) canola oil
1 shallot, minced
1 cup (250 mL) sour cherries, pitted
2 oz (60 mL) ruby port
1/4 cup (60 mL) brown sugar
1 tbsp (15 mL) soy sauce
1/2 cup (125 mL) duck, chicken OR
    beef stock
1 pinch dried chiles
salt and pepper, to taste

● ● ● ●

Brine: Combine all brine ingredients in a large pail or stockpot. Place duck in brine. Place a pie plate or a clean brick on duck to immerse. Let duck sit in brine, refrigerated, for 1 day or up to 3 days. Remove duck from brine and pat dry. If you have time, let duck sit in refrigerator, uncovered, on a draining rack for an additional day.

Duck: Prepare Bradley Stainless Steel smoker following manufacturer's directions. Add cherry wood bisquettes to the smoke generator and smoke for approximately 1 1/2 to 2 hours. Remove duck from smoker and preheat oven to 375°F (190°C). Bake duck until internal temperature reaches 140°F (60°C), or until desired doneness.

Sauce: Heat oil in a skillet over medium-high heat; sauté shallot. Add cherries and continue to sauté; deglaze with port. Add remaining ingredients and simmer at a low boil until reduced to a syrupy consistency.

Remove duck breasts and cut on an angle into thin slices; fan in centre of each of 2 plates. Dollop sour cherry sauce on top and serve with a julienne of carrot, radish and vermicelli rice noodles.

● ● ● ●

SERVES 2 TO 4

Recipe by chef Alex Svenne
Photography: Brian Gould

Pair With:
• Californian Pinot Noir
• Australian Cabernet-Merlot

Sugar & Spice Cured Turkey

20 lb (9 kg) turkey
3 large white onions, cut horizontally into 3/4" (2 cm) slices
1 cup (250 mL) packed Demerara sugar
1/2 cup (125 mL) kosher salt
4 tsp (20 mL) onion powder
2 tsp (10 mL) garlic powder
2 tsp (10 mL) ground allspice
2 tsp (10 mL) ground cloves
2 tsp (10 mL) ground mace
2 tsp (10 mL) ground black pepper
3 cups (750 mL) chicken broth

● ● ● ●

Rinse turkey inside and out; pat dry with paper towels. Line the bottom of a large roasting pan with onion slices. Place cleaned turkey in the centre of 2 sheets of waxed paper. In a small bowl, combine sugar, salt, onion powder, garlic powder, allspice, cloves, mace and pepper; place spice mixture in a shaker. Sprinkle spice mixture all over outside of turkey. Let sit 10 minutes. Repeat. Once completely covered in spice mixture, place turkey on top of onion slices in roasting pan. Place in refrigerator, uncovered, for 24 hours.

Once finished curing for 24 hours, remove turkey from refrigerator. Place oven rack in lowest position and preheat oven to 325°F (160°C). Tie legs together and tuck wings under turkey. Cover loosely with foil.

Roast turkey 2 hours. Uncover and roast 30 minutes. Add 1 1/2 cups (375 mL) broth to roasting pan; baste turkey with broth. Roast turkey 1 hour, basting occasionally. Add 1 1/2 cups (375 mL) broth to roasting pan; continue to roast turkey until dark brown, basting with broth every 15 minutes, about 1 hour. Increase temperature to 375°C (190°F) and cover turkey loosely with foil; continue to roast, approximately 1 1/2 hours, or until an instant-read thermometer inserted into innermost part of thigh registers 180°F (83°C).

Remove turkey from oven and tent with foil; let stand 30 minutes. Carve and serve immediately.

● ● ● ●

Recipe by Brandon Boone
Photography: Brian Gould

Garlic & Olive Oil Marinated Lamb Skewers

2 lb (1 kg) boneless lamb loin
1 cup (250 mL) olive pomace oil*
1 tbsp (15 mL) minced garlic
1 tbsp (15 mL) salt
1 tsp (5 mL) black pepper
2 lbs (1 kg) bell peppers, red, green and yellow
1 lb (500 g) red onions
1 zucchini
1 lb (500 g) button mushrooms
6, 8" (20 cm) skewers

Garlic Chile Glaze:

1/4 cup (60 mL) butter, room temperature
1 tsp (5 mL) Piri Piri dried chiles OR red chiles flakes
1 tsp (5 mL) minced garlic
2 tbsp (30 mL) white wine
salt and pepper, to taste
1 tsp (5 mL) minced fresh Italian parsley
rosemary sprigs

Remove excess fat from lamb loin and cut into 1" (2.5 cm) cubes. Combine oil, garlic, salt and pepper in a bowl; mix well. Add lamb to bowl and mix to coat well. Cover bowl with plastic wrap and refrigerate for 1 hour.

Cut bell peppers, onions and zucchini into 1" (2.5 cm) cubes; leave mushrooms whole. Begin preparing skewers by alternating vegetables with lamb (3 to 4 pieces of lamb per skewer) until all ingredients are used.

Glaze: In a mixing bowl, combine all ingredients, except rosemary; whisk well.

On an open grill or barbecue set over high heat, place skewers on the cooking surface. Grill for 1 minute; flip and grill remaining sides until cooked (to medium doneness is ideal); brush with glaze. Before serving, top with rosemary sprigs.

* olive pomace oil is produced from the residue of the production of grade B olive oil with the pits

SERVES 3

Recipe by chef Richard Duncan

Photography: Brian Gould

Pair With:
• Italian Barolo
• Australian Shiraz
• Washington State Syrah

Lamb Chops with Roasted Pepper & Tomato Sauce with Charred Onions & Bourbon

Make this surprisingly rich sauce in late summer, when the vegetables are prolific and the onions are sweet.

Roasted Pepper & Tomato Sauce with Charred Onions & Bourbon:

1 dried ancho OR morita chile
1 tbsp (15 mL) extra-virgin olive oil
5–6 ripe tomatoes, halved
1 onion, sliced lengthwise
1 head of garlic, root trimmed, paper left on
2 red bell peppers
1/2 tsp (2.5 mL) dried oregano
1 tbsp (15 mL) honey
juice and grated zest of 1 lemon
salt and hot chile flakes, to taste
2 tbsp (30 mL) minced fresh basil
1 tbsp (15 mL) minced fresh thyme OR chives
bourbon, to taste

4, 6 oz (170 g) bone-in lamb chops
olive oil

● ● ● ○

Sauce: Put chile into a small pot with water to cover. Bring to a simmer and cook until tender. Lightly oil cut surfaces of tomatoes, onion, garlic and peppers; grill until the vegetables are lightly charred and tender. Transfer grilled vegetables to a food processor and chop as coarsely as you like. Stir in oregano, honey and lemon juice. Balance flavours with salt and hot chile flakes. Add ancho chile and purée into a fine sauce texture. Add bourbon to taste.

Preheat a gas grill or charcoal barbecue. Season lamb chops with salt and pepper and brush with oil. Place on grill and cook over low heat for 5 to 7 minutes a side, or until desired doneness. Remove from heat and spoon sauce on before serving.

● ● ● ○

SERVES 4

Recipe by dee Hobsbawn-Smith

Photography: Brian Gould

Pair With:
• Barbaresco
• Washington State Syrah
• South African Pinotage

Herb Encrusted Rack of Lamb with Port-Red Wine Sauce

Port-Red Wine Sauce:
1 1/2 cups (375 mL) dry red wine
3/4 cup (175 mL) tawny port
1/2 cup (125 mL) butter, divided into
  8 individual, equal portions
salt and pepper, to taste

1/4 cup (60 mL) panko*
3/4 cup (175 mL) chopped fresh parsley
2 tsp (10 mL) chopped fresh rosemary
1 tsp (5 mL) chopped fresh thyme
1 tsp (5 mL) finely grated lemon zest
2 garlic cloves
2, 1 lb (500 g) racks of lamb, fat trimmed
salt and pepper, to taste
2 tbsp (30 mL) olive oil
1/3 cup (75 mL) Dijon mustard

● ● ● ●

Sauce: In a large saucepan over medium-high heat, combine red wine and port; boil until reduced to 1/3 cup (75 mL), approximately 25 minutes. Remove from heat. Add butter, 1 portion at a time, whisking until melted. Season with salt and pepper and drizzle on lamb before serving.

Preheat oven to 350°F (180°C). Place panko on a baking sheet. Bake until lightly toasted, approximately 5 minutes. Remove from oven and let cool. Combine panko, herbs, lemon zest and garlic in a food processor; process until well incorporated. Place panko mixture in a bowl and chill.

Preheat oven to 425°F (220°C). Season lamb with salt and pepper. Heat oil in a large heavy skillet over high heat; add lamb and brown well, turning occasionally, approximately 10 minutes. Remove lamb from skillet and transfer to a baking pan. Roast lamb for approximately 15 minutes, or until it reaches an internal temperature of 130°F (54°C). Remove from oven and let rest for 10 minutes. Using a pastry brush, coat lamb with mustard; dredge in panko mixture, coating completely, Return lamb to baking pan and roast until panko mixture appears dry. Remove lamb from oven and let rest 5 minutes at room temperature.

* **Panko** is coarse bread crumbs used in Japanese cooking for coating fried foods. Generally sold in Asian supermarkets or in health-food stores.

● ● ● ●

SERVES 4

Recipe by Brandon Boone
Photography: Brian Gould

Pair With:
• Australian Grenache
• Chateauneuf du Pape
• Naramata Bench Syrah

ⓇRack of Canadian Lamb with Honey & Wheat Flakes

Balsamic Au Jus:
1 1/2 lbs (680 g) lamb bones and scraps*
3 oz (85 g) mushrooms, chopped
1 onion, peeled and chopped
handful thyme, bay leaf and stems from parsley
1 cup (250 mL) red wine
6 cups (1.5 L) veal stock
1/2 cup (125 mL) aged balsamic vinegar
salt and pepper, to taste

Garlic Roasted Red Pepper Mashed Potatoes:
1 tsp (5 mL) canola oil
2 garlic cloves, minced
3 large whole peeled potatoes, cooked
1 tbsp (15 mL) unsalted butter
1 tbsp (15 mL) whipping cream
1/2 red bell pepper, roasted, peeled and puréed
1 tsp (5 mL) EACH, chopped fresh parsley, thyme and chives
salt and pepper, to taste

Rack of Lamb:
1 cup (250 mL) wheat flakes
2 racks of lamb, about 6–8 bones each, chine bone removed
salt and freshly ground pepper, to taste
1/3 cup (75 mL) liquid honey
1/2 cup (125 mL) chopped fresh herbs such as chervil, parsley, chives
   and rosemary

Rack of Canadian Lamb with Honey & Wheat Flakes (continued)

● ● ● ●

Balsamic Au Jus: Place bones and scraps in a heavy-bottomed saucepan over medium heat. Add mushrooms, onion and herbs. Sauté for 5 minutes to add colour. Add wine and bring to a boil; reduce heat and simmer until about 1/4 cup (60 mL) remains. Add stock; bring to a boil; reduce and let cook at a slow simmer until reduced to 2 cups (500 mL), about 45 minutes. Add vinegar and cook for 2 minutes. Season with salt and pepper; remove from heat and strain. Set aside to keep warm.

Potatoes: Heat oil in a small skillet over low heat and gently sauté garlic until browned and soft, about 5 to 7 minutes. Mash cooked potatoes with garlic, butter and cream. Fold in puréed roasted red peppers and chopped parsley, thyme and chives. Season with salt and pepper to taste.

Lamb: Preheat oven to 350°F (180°C). Spread wheat flakes on a baking sheet and toast for 10 minutes, stirring occasionally. Remove from oven to cool.

In a large lightly oiled skillet over high heat, sear lamb racks until browned, about 3 to 4 minutes. Season with salt and pepper. Brush meaty side with honey and place, basted side up, in a shallow open roasting pan.

In a medium bowl, combine cooled wheat flakes, remaining honey and herbs. Pat honey mixture onto meaty portion of lamb racks. Roast about 12 to15 minutes, or until medium-rare and internal temperature registers 145°F (62°C) on a meat thermometer. Remove and transfer to a platter; cover loosely and let rest 15 minutes.

With a piping bag, make a tower of potatoes in the centre of the plate. Cut lamb between the bones to make individual chops. Arrange 3 to 4 chops around potato tower. Drizzle with Balsamic au Jus.

*can be obtained from your butcher

● ● ● ●

SERVES 4

Recipe by chef Leo Pantel
Photography: Patricia Holdsworth

Pair With:
• Chilean Cabernet Sauvignon
• French Beaujolais
• Spanish Rioja

Lamb Racks with Coriander Pesto

Coriander Pesto:
1 cup (250 mL) packed fresh cilantro
1/4 cup (60 mL) extra-virgin olive oil
2 tbsp (30 mL) pine nuts
1 tsp (5 mL) grated lemon zest
1 tsp (5 mL) lemon juice
1 tsp (5 mL) balsamic vinegar
2 tbsp (30 mL) grated Parmesan cheese
1 small garlic clove, minced
1/4 tsp (1 mL) EACH, salt and pepper

Lamb Racks:
2 racks of lamb (about 2 lbs/1 kg) backbone removed

● ● ● ○

Pesto: In a mini chopper or food processor, process coriander, oil, pine nuts, lemon zest, juice and balsamic vinegar until smooth, adding up to 1 tbsp (15 mL) more oil if necessary to thin. Scrape into bowl. Stir in cheese, garlic, salt and pepper. Set aside. (NOTE: Pesto can be covered with plastic wrap and refrigerated for up to 24 hours. Bring to room temperature before continuing.)

Lamb: Place lamb racks on a plate. Spread pesto over fatty side of both racks. Let stand at room temperature for 30 minutes. Place racks, fatty side up, on a greased grill set over medium-high heat; cook for 20 to 25 minutes, or until a meat thermometer registers 140°F (60°C) for rare, or until desired doneness. When a grill is not available, cook on the rack of a small roasting pan, fatty side up, in 425°F (220°C) oven for 20 to 25 minutes.

Remove to cutting board and tent with foil; let stand for 10 minutes. Carve into single portions.

● ● ● ○

SERVES 4

Recipe by Daphna Rabinovitch
Photography: Brian Gould

Ginger-Skewered Pork & Pineapple

several pieces of fresh ginger, 4" (10 cm) in length
2 tbsp (30 mL) mango chutney
1 tbsp (15 mL) Dijon mustard
1 tbsp (15 mL) peanut oil
1 pork tenderloin, silver skin removed, cut into 1/4" (6 mm) slices
1/2 pineapple, peeled, cored and cut into bite-sized pieces
2 ripe nectarines, pitted and cut into bite-sized pieces
2 plums, pitted and cut into bite-sized pieces
2 tbsp (30 mL) butter, melted
1 tsp (5 mL) ground ginger

● ● ● ○

Peel fresh ginger and cut into several 4" (10 cm) long skewers. Using a vegetable peeler or knife, carve ginger into a sharp point on one end. Depending on the size of the ginger, continue to make skewers until you have 12 good pieces.

In a mixing bowl, combine mango chutney, mustard and oil; whisk well. Place pork slices in mango mixture, turning to coat evenly; let marinate for 1 hour. Preheat a gas grill. Thread pork slices and fruit alternately on ginger skewers. In a small bowl, mix melted butter and ground ginger; brush fruit with butter mixture. Place on barbecue and grill for about 4 minutes each side. Remove from heat and serve immediately.

● ● ● ○

SERVES 4

Recipe by Brandon Boone
Photography: Brian Gould

Pair With:
• Junmai Sake
• B.C. Semillon
• Chilean Sauvignon Blanc

Grilled Garlic Lime Pork Tenderloin with Mango Chutney

Marinade:
6 large garlic cloves, chopped
2 tbsp (30 mL) soy sauce
2 tbsp (30 mL) grated fresh ginger
1 tbsp (15 mL) Dijon mustard
1/3 cup (75 mL) lime juice
1/2 cup (125 mL) olive oil
salt and pepper, to taste
2 pieces of star anise

2 trimmed pork tenderloins

Mango Chutney:
1 1/2 lbs (750 g) slightly underripe mangoes, peeled, coarsely chopped
2 garlic cloves, minced
1 tbsp (15 mL) grated fresh ginger
1/2 tsp (2 mL) ground cinnamon
pinch of cloves
1/2 tsp (2 mL) kosher salt
1/4 cup (60 mL) sugar
1 cup (250 mL) cider vinegar
1 tsp (5 mL) chile paste

● ● ● ○

Marinade: Combine all ingredients, except salt, pepper and star anise, in a food processor; blend and season with salt and pepper. In a resealable plastic bag combine marinade, star anise and pork. Place in a shallow baking dish and refrigerate for 1 day, turning occasionally, or up to 2 days.

Chutney: In a saucepan set over medium-high heat, combine all ingredients and bring to a boil. Reduce heat and let simmer for 1 hour, stirring occasionally. Remove from heat and let cool before serving. (Makes 3 cups/750 mL)

Preheat a barbecue. Remove pork from marinade and let stand at room temperature for approximately 30 minutes before grilling. Cook on a lightly greased grill for 15 to 20 minutes, turning occasionally. Remove from heat and let sit 5 minutes before slicing.

● ● ● ○

SERVES 4

Recipe by Brandon Boone
Photography: Brian Gould

Pair With:
• California Chardonnay
• Okanagan Valley Viognier

Curry-Brined Baby Back Ribs
with Apricot Barbecue Sauce

Basic Brine:
4 qts (4 L) cold water
1 cup (250 mL) EACH, salt and brown sugar
3 bay leaves
1 1/2 tbsp (22 mL) whole peppercorns

Curry Brine:
1 recipe basic brine (see above)
1/4 cup (60 mL) curry powder
1 tbsp (15 mL) EACH, cumin and coriander seeds
1 tbsp (15 mL) dried chile flakes, more/less to taste
2 limes, cut in half (squeeze into the brine, then throw the lime halves in)

4 racks baby back ribs

Apricot Barbecue Sauce:
10 fresh apricots, peeled, pitted and
    diced or 1 cup (250 mL) dried, diced
    and soaked in water overnight
1 tbsp (15 mL) canola oil
1 tsp (15 mL) minced fresh ginger
1 tsp (15 mL) minced garlic
1 onion, finely diced
1 tsp (5 mL) chile flakes
juice and grated zest of 1 lime
1/4 cup (60 mL) vinegar
1/4 cup (60 mL) brown sugar
1 tsp (5 mL) salt
1 cup (250 mL) water

● ● ● ○

Basic Brine: Combine all ingredients in a large stockpot. Stir until salt and brown sugar dissolve. Make sure to make enough brine to completely immerse whatever you are planning to put in. Top with a weight (a dinner plate works well) to keep the food fully immersed. Cover and refrigerate for 24 hours or up to 3 days. Remove from brine and rinse.

Curry Brine: Combine all ingredients in a large pot. Cover and refrigerate for 24 hours or up to 3 days. Remove from brine and rinse ribs.

Sauce: Heat oil in a skillet over medium-high heat; add onion, ginger and garlic. Sauté until onion is translucent. Add remaining ingredients and bring to a boil. Simmer until thick.

Preheat a gas or charcoal barbecue to low. Grill ribs on barbecue until cooked. Brush with sauce before serving.

● ● ● ○

SERVES 4

Recipe by chef Alex Svenne

Photography: Brian Gould

Pair With:
• Hungarian Pinot Gris
• Alsatian Gewürztraminer
• B.C. Chenin Blanc

Raspberry Chipotle Ribs

Try these recipes to recreate the flavours of cowboy country at home or to take on your next trail ride or adventure at the cabin.

Seasoned Stock:
10 cups (2.5 L) water or enough to cover ribs
4 cups (1 L) cola
1/2 cup (125 mL) fresh thyme sprigs
1/2 cup (125 mL) fresh rosemary sprigs
2 tbsp (30 mL) pickling spice
juice of 3 lemons
1 tsp (5 mL) salt
1/4 cup (60 mL) Worcestershire sauce
1 tsp (5 mL) thinly sliced hot chile pepper

2 lbs (1 kg) pork side ribs

Raspberry Chipotle Sauce:
2 cups (500 g) raspberries
2 tbsp (30 mL) Tabasco chipotle sauce, or to taste
1/2 cup (125 mL) extra-virgin olive oil
2 tbsp (30 mL) brown sugar

● ● ● ○

Stock: In a large stockpot over medium-high heat, combine water, cola, thyme, rosemary, pickling spice, lemon juice, salt, Worcestershire sauce and chile pepper; bring to a boil. Add ribs, reduce heat to a simmer and cook ribs 1 1/2 hours, or until tender; remove and let cool to room temperature.

Sauce: In a blender, combine all ingredients; purée until smooth.

Preheat oven to 300°F (150°C) or prepare a barbecue. Brush ribs with sauce and bake for 10 to 15 minutes or grill, using indirect heat, until sauce browns.

● ● ● ○

SERVES 4

Recipe by chef Craig Guenther
Photography: Brian Gould

Pair With:
• Italian Barolo
• Californian Zinfandel
• Spanish Sauvignon Blanc

(W)hiskey Apple Prosciutto al Forno

Apple Cider Marinade:
1 cup (250 mL) apple cider
juice of 1 lemon
4 bay leaves
1 tbsp (15 mL) fresh rosemary
  leaves
3 tbsp (45 mL) brown sugar
1 tbsp (15 mL) dry mustard
3 garlic cloves, roughly
  chopped

4 lb (2 kg) partially cooked
  bone-in ham
1 1/2 cups (375 mL) whiskey
  (such as Jack Daniel's)
1 cup (250 mL) chicken stock
2 tbsp (30 mL) flour
2 tbsp (30 mL) butter
salt and pepper, to taste

● ● ● ○

Marinade: In a saucepan over medium-low heat, combine cider, lemon juice, bay leaves, rosemary, sugar, mustard and garlic; stir until sugar is dissolved. Remove from heat and let cool. Place ham in a large resealable bag and add marinade; seal and turn to coat evenly. Refrigerate for 12 hours, turning every couple of hours.

Preheat oven to 350°F (180°C). Place ham and marinade in a roasting pan; cover with aluminum foil and bake 1 hour, turning occasionally. Remove foil and brush ham with whiskey every 15 minutes, for an additional hour.

Remove ham from pan and place on a rack to cool. Skim excess fat from pan and place pan over low heat. Add chicken stock; stirring up browned bits from bottom of pan. Turn heat to medium-high and whisk in flour and butter until pan juices thicken to form gravy. Season with salt and pepper.

Slice ham and serve immediately with gravy.

● ● ● ○

SERVES 6

Recipe by Brandon Boone
Photography: Brian Gould

Pair With:
• Hunter Valley Semillon
• California Sangiovese
• Chianti

ambalaya

1/4 cup (60 mL) vegetable oil
2 green peppers, chopped
2 white onions, chopped
6 celery stalks, chopped
1 tbsp (15 mL) minced garlic
1 lb (500 g) smoked ham, diced
4 chorizo links, cooked and sliced
4 andouille links, cooked and sliced
19 oz (540 mL) can whole plum tomatoes, mashed by hand
1 1/2 cups (375 mL) long-grain rice
1/4 cup (60 mL) hot sauce
1/4 cup (60 mL) Cajun spice
pinch of salt
1 cup (250 mL) water
1/4 lb (125 g) shrimp for garnish (optional)

● ● ● ●

Heat oil in a large skillet over medium heat. Add peppers, onions, celery and garlic; sauté until onions are translucent. Add ham and sausages to pan and cook for 5 minutes, stirring occasionally. Add tomatoes, rice, hot sauce, Cajun spice, salt and water. Bring to a boil then reduce to a simmer. Cook until rice is soft. Add shrimp for last 4 to 5 minutes. Remove from heat and serve immediately.

● ● ● ●

SERVES 4

Recipe by chef Darcy Fry

Photography: Hamid Attie Photography

Pair With:
• Côtes du Ventoux Rosé
• B.C. Pinot Gris
• Australian Viognier

Pan-Seared Provimi Veal Chop with Raspberry Sauce

Raspberry Sauce:
1 cup (250 mL) veal
    OR beef stock
1/3 cup (75 mL)
    raspberry jelly
1 tsp (5 mL) cornstarch
1/4 cup (60 mL) EACH,
    raspberry vinegar
    and port wine
salt and pepper, to
    taste

4, 10 oz (285 mL) veal
    chops
salt and pepper, to
    taste
vegetable oil for frying

● ● ● ○

Sauce: In a medium saucepan over medium heat, bring veal stock to a simmer. Add raspberry jelly and gently boil for 5 minutes to dissolve jelly. In a small bowl, mix cornstarch with raspberry vinegar until dissolved. Slowly incorporate cornstarch mixture into hot veal stock. Add port wine and simmer until sauce thickens. Add salt and pepper to taste.

Preheat oven to 350°F (180°C). Season veal chops lightly with salt and pepper. Heat oil in a skillet over medium-high heat. Sear chops in skillet until brown on each side. Place on a heatproof platter and bake for 15 minutes, or until desired doneness.

To serve, top veal chops with raspberry sauce. Serve immediately.

● ● ● ○

SERVES 4

Recipe by chef Albertino Costa

Photography: Brian Gould

Pair With:
• Oregon Pinot Noir
• Beaujolais Cru
• California Zinfandel

 # Osso Bucco

5 lbs (2.25 kg) veal shank
kosher salt and freshly cracked black pepper
2 tbsp (30 mL) olive oil
2 carrots, diced
2 Spanish onions, diced
2 celery stalks, diced
1/2 cup (125 mL) fresh thyme
2 bay leaves
3 cups (750 mL) dry white wine
1 1/2 cups (375 mL) EACH, chicken stock and veal stock
3 cups (750 mL) tomato sauce

● ● ● ●

Preheat oven to 375°F (190°C). Season shanks with salt and pepper. Heat oil over medium-high heat in a pan until smoking. Brown shanks, a few at a time; remove and keep warm. Reduce heat to medium; add carrots, onions, celery, thyme and bay leaves; cook until golden brown. Add wine, stock and tomato sauce and bring to a boil. Return shanks to the pan, making sure they are submerged at least halfway, if not add more stock. Cover tightly with aluminum foil. Place in oven and braise for 2 hours. Remove foil and cook another 30 minutes, until meat is close to falling off the bone.

● ● ● ●

SERVES 4

Recipe by chef Kevin Lendrum
Photography: John Ulan/Epic Photography

Pair With:
• Italian Brunello di Montalcino
• California Cabernet Sauvignon
• Spanish Rioja Reserva

Seared Beef Tenderloin in Merlot Shiitake Sauce

2 tbsp (30 mL) butter
4, 6 oz (170 g) beef tenderloin steaks
kosher salt and freshly ground pepper

Merlot Shiitake Sauce:
5 garlic cloves, minced
1/2 cup (125 mL) chopped shallots
8 oz (250 g) shiitake mushrooms
2 tsp (10 mL) dried thyme
2 cups (500 mL) Merlot, divided
2 cups (500 mL) beef stock
1 tbsp (15 mL) cornstarch
1 tbsp (15 mL) water

● ● ● ○

Preheat oven to 375°F (190°C).

Melt butter in an ovenproof skillet over medium-high heat. Season tenderloin with salt and pepper and add to skillet. Sear each piece on both sides for 1 to 2 minutes, or until browned. Place skillet in oven and cook until desired doneness.

Sauce: In a separate skillet, melt butter over medium-high heat. Add garlic and shallots to skillet and sauté for 1 to 2 minutes. Add mushrooms and thyme; continue to sauté until mushrooms are lightly browned and tender. Deglaze pan with 1/4 cup (60 mL) of Merlot. Add beef stock and remaining wine to skillet; bring to a boil then reduce heat to a simmer. Let sauce simmer for 10 minutes. In a small bowl, mix cornstarch and water. Add cornstarch mixture to sauce and stir to incorporate. Simmer an additional 5 minutes, stirring occasionally. Season sauce with salt and pepper; cover and remove from heat.

Remove tenderloins from oven and place on 4 plates. Spoon sauce over and serve immediately.

● ● ● ○

SERVES 4

Recipe by Brandon Boone

Pair With:
• French Merlot
• Australian Shiraz
• India Pale Ale

Ginger-Garlic Flank Steak with Grilled Green Onions

Ginger-Garlic Marinade:
1 tbsp (5 mL) finely minced ginger
3 garlic cloves, minced
1 tsp (5 mL) whole peppercorns, coarsely ground
1 tsp (5 mL) sea salt
1/4 cup (60 mL) EACH, soy sauce, sesame oil and rice wine vinegar
2 tbsp (30 mL) honey

2, 1 lb (500 g) flank steaks
2 bunches green onions
1 tbsp (15 mL) olive oil

● ● ● ●

Marinade: Combine ginger, garlic, pepper, salt, soy sauce, sesame oil, vinegar and honey in a bowl; mix well. Combine steaks and marinade in a resealable plastic bag; seal and shake. Marinate in the refrigerator for 1 to 2 hours, turning every 30 minutes.

Remove steak from bag and discard marinade. Preheat a gas grill. Cook steaks on barbecue until desired doneness. Just prior to removing steaks from barbecue, brush green onions with oil and sprinkle with salt and pepper. Place on grill for 1 minute; flip onions and cook for 1 minute longer. Remove from heat. Slice steak into thin strips and top with sliced green onions.

● ● ● ●

SERVES 2

Recipe by Brandon Boone

Photography: Brian Gould

Pair With:
• B.C. Gamay Noir
• Valpolicella
• Red Burgundy

unslinger Striploin

Gunslinger Rub:
2 tsp (10 mL) ground chipotle pepper OR chili powder
1 tsp (5 mL) cocoa
1/2 tsp (2 mL) ground cinnamon
2 tsp (10 mL) instant espresso powder
1 tbsp (15 mL) brown sugar
1 tsp (5 mL) kosher salt
1 tsp (5 mL) freshly ground pepper

2, 1 lb (500 g) striploin steaks

● ● ● ●

Rub: Combine all ingredients, in a bowl; mix well.

Place spice mixture in a shaker and sprinkle all over both sides of steaks. Let rest at room temperature for 15 minutes.

Preheat a gas barbecue. Grill steaks until desired doneness. Remove from heat and let stand for 5 minutes before serving.

● ● ● ●

SERVES 2

Recipe by Brandon Boone
Photography: Brian Gould

Pair With:
• Washington State Merlot
• Australian Shiraz
• California Petite Sirah

Beef Short Ribs with Espresso Java Sauce

Short ribs used to be the poor cousins of the rib family, relegated to soups and stews. Short ribs have come of age and I salute their newfound status. Whether you call them beef short ribs or simmering short ribs, these can tackle almost any flavour combination and come out tender, delicious and appealing.

Espresso Java Sauce:
1 tbsp (15 mL) vegetable oil
1 small onion, finely chopped
2 garlic cloves, minced
2 tbsp (30 mL) espresso powder OR coffee granules
1 tbsp (15 mL) EACH, chili powder, paprika and salt
2 tsp (10 mL) ground cumin
1/2 tsp (2 mL) EACH, cinnamon and ground ginger
3/4 cup (175 mL) boiling water
1/4 cup (60 mL) EACH, chili sauce and fancy molasses
1/4 cup (60 mL) packed brown sugar
1 tbsp (15 mL) cider vinegar
2 tsp (10 mL) Worcestershire sauce
3 lbs (1.5 kg) lean beef Miami-cut short ribs

Beef Short Ribs with Espresso Java Sauce
(continued)

● ● ● ○

Sauce: In a skillet over medium heat, heat oil. Add onion and garlic; cook, stirring for 3 minutes, or until softened. Add espresso powder, chili powder, paprika, salt, cumin, cinnamon and ginger. Cook, stirring, for 1 minute. Pour in boiling water, chili sauce, molasses, sugar, vinegar and Worcestershire sauce; bring to a boil. Reduce heat and boil gently for 5 to 10 minutes, or until reduced to 1 cup (250 mL). Cool slightly.

Arrange ribs, slightly overlapping, in a 9 x 13" (23 x 33 cm) baking dish. Pour espresso sauce over. Cover and refrigerate for at least 4 hours or for up to 24 hours. Bring to room temperature.

Divide ribs between 3 large pieces of aluminum foil, spreading any remaining sauce evenly over. Loosely wrap foil over ribs and seal packages tightly.

Place packages on a preheated grill set over medium-low heat or in a 325°F (160°C) oven on a rimmed baking sheet; grill or roast for 1 to 1 1/2 hours, or until meat is tender. Unwrap ribs and serve.

If a more crispy texture is desired, ribs can then be placed directly on a medium-high grill for 6 to 10 minutes.

● ● ● ○

SERVES 4

Recipe by Daphna Rabinovitch
Photography: Brian Gould

Pair With:
• Italian Barola
• Okanagan Cabernet Sauvignon

 raised Short Ribs with Baco Noir & Black Plums

Baco Noir is a hybrid grape popular with Canadian winemakers as it was developed for cold weather hardiness. It makes a dark, plum-coloured wine with lots of flavour. A good choice to pair with big-game meats such as bison, elk or deer is the Henry of Pelham Baco Noir.

4 lbs (2 kg) short ribs, ask a butcher for "English cut"

Baco Noir Marinade:
2 cups (500 mL) Baco Noir (This will leave 1 cup/250 mL in the bottle for you to drink while cooking)
1 medium onion, diced
1 tomato, diced
1 sprig fresh rosemary OR 1 tsp (5 mL) dried
2 garlic cloves, crushed
1/4 cup (60 mL) canola oil
1 tsp (5 mL) EACH, black pepper and salt

Seasoned Flour:
2 cups (500 mL) all-purpose flour
1/4 cup (60 mL) paprika
1 tbsp (15 mL) EACH, salt and pepper
1 tsp (5 mL) cayenne pepper

Braise:
1/4 cup (60 mL) canola oil
1 cup (250 mL) shallots, peeled but not chopped
2 large carrots, peeled and cut into bite-sized pieces
1 large sweet potato, peeled and cut into bite-sized pieces
6 black plums, pitted and quartered
1 cinnamon stick
4–6 whole cloves
2 cups (500 mL) beef stock OR 10 oz (284 mL) can beef consommé
pinch of chile flakes
salt and pepper, to taste

● ● ● ○

Marinade: Combine all marinade ingredients in a pot and bring to a boil, simmer for about 10 minutes. Cool completely.

Put ribs in a casserole or a bowl. Pour marinade over ribs and toss to coat completely. Let marinate for 4 hours or overnight. Turn ribs over a couple of times to make sure they are evenly marinated.

Drain off marinade and reserve. Pat ribs with paper towel to dry. Dredge ribs in seasoned flour to coat evenly. Shake off excess flour.

(B)raised Short Ribs with Baco Noir & Black Plums *(continued)*

In a heavy-bottomed pot or Dutch oven, heat oil over medium-high heat. Working in small batches, brown short ribs, turning to brown all sides. You need a nice dark brown colour to achieve the best flavour. If the oil starts to smoke or the flour burns, turn down the heat. Don't try to brown too many ribs at once; they won't brown properly. There should be spaces between each rib in the pot. When ribs are browned, remove from pot and set aside.

Place shallots in the pot and sauté until soft. Add reserved marinade and bring to a boil. Add carrots, sweet potatoes, plums, cinnamon stick, cloves, beef stock and chile flakes. Bring to a low boil.

Return ribs to pot and reduce heat to a simmer. Partially cover pot and simmer for 2 hours. The meat should be falling-off-the-bone tender. (For bison or game meats you will only need 1 1/2 hours.) Put the pot in a 300°F (150°C) oven for 2 hours. You could also put this in a slow cooker in the morning to enjoy when you get home from work.

Serve with a big pile of creamy mashed potatoes, egg noodles tossed in butter or a wild rice pilaf. This recipe is great made the day before and reheated.

● ● ● ●

SERVES 4

Recipe by chef Alex Svenne
Photography: Brian Gould

Southwest Brined Brisket with Chipotle Barbecue Sauce

Southwest Brine:
1 recipe Basic Brine, page 181
1 tbsp (15 mL) cumin seeds
2 limes, cut in half (squeeze into brine, then throw lime halves in)
1 chipotle pepper
1 jalapeño, cut in half
1 tbsp (15 mL) chili powder
3 garlic cloves, cut in half
1 onion, quartered
cilantro stems (leaves used in sauce)
2 lb (1 kg) brisket

Chipotle Barbecue Sauce:
1 tbsp (15 mL) canola oil
1 onion, diced
1 tbsp (15 mL) minced garlic
3 chipotle peppers in adobo sauce, chopped
1 tbsp (15 mL) chili powder
1 tsp (5 mL) ground cumin
1/2 cup (125 mL) brown sugar
1/2 cup (125 mL) EACH, vinegar and strong brewed coffee
1 cup (250 mL) diced tomato
1 cup (250 mL) ketchup
juice and zest of 2 limes
1 tbsp (15 mL) minced cilantro leaves

● ● ● ○

Brine: Combine all ingredients in a large stockpot. Stir until salt and brown sugar dissolve. Make sure to make enough brine to completely immerse whatever you are planning to put in. Then put a weight (a dinner plate works well) to keep the food fully immersed. Cover and refrigerate for 24 hours or up to 3 days. Remove from brine and rinse.

Sauce: Heat oil in a skillet over medium-high heat; sauté onions, garlic and peppers. Add remaining ingredients and bring to a boil; simmer until thickened.

Prepare a gas or charcoal barbecue for offset cooking. Place brisket in an aluminum roasting pan and cook on barbecue over low heat for 3 hours, flipping every hour. Remove from heat, tent with foil and let rest for 10 minutes. Remove foil and slice brisket into thin strips. Toss with Chipotle Barbecue Sauce and serve with crusty buns.

● ● ● ○

SERVES 6

Recipe by chef Alex Svenne

Photography: Brian Gould

Pair With:
• California Zinfandel
• Australian Shiraz
• South of France Merlot

(B)elgian Dark Beer Stew

2 lbs (1 kg) stewing beef
1 cup (250 mL) diced onion, divided
1/2 cup (125 mL) celery, finely chopped
1/2 bottle of dark beer
1 tbsp (15 mL) vinegar
2 bay leaves
1/2 tsp (2 mL) horseradish
1/4 tsp (1 mL) EACH, dry mustard and seasoning salt
sprinkling of thyme
salt and pepper, to taste
1 tbsp (15 mL) cornstarch

● ● ● ●

In a large pot over medium-high heat, brown beef with 1/2 cup (125 mL) onion. Add remaining onion and remaining ingredients, except cornstarch, to pot. Add 1/2 cup (125 mL) to 3/4 cup (175 mL) water, enough to cover beef. Simmer, covered, until beef is tender. Mix cornstarch with a small amount of water to prevent lumping; add to pot; continue to cook until stew has thickened to desired consistency.

Serve with a light salad, with fries and mayonnaise on the side.

● ● ● ●

Recipe courtesy of Angele Thienpondt and Anna Boel
Photography: Brian Gould

Pair With:
• Pale Ale
• Bitter Ale
• Porter

Beef Carbonade

3 lbs (1.5 kg) flank steak, cut into 1 1/2" (4 cm) cubes
6 shallots, thinly sliced
5 garlic cloves, crushed
1 lb (500 g) porcini mushrooms, quartered
2 jalapeños, cored, seeded, cut in half and thinly sliced
3 large carrots, peeled and cut into 1/2" (1.3 cm) rounds
2 leeks, white part only, sliced
2 tbsp (30 mL) Dijon mustard
1 tbsp (15 mL) brown sugar
2 cups (500 mL) Flemish beer OR other dark beer
2 cups (500 mL) beef stock
1/2 cup (125 mL) Shiraz OR other good-quality red wine
2 tbsp (30 mL) balsamic vinegar
2 bay leaves
1/2 cup (125 mL) chopped fresh parsley
1 tbsp (15 mL) dried thyme
2 tsp (10 mL) EACH, kosher salt and freshly ground pepper
2 tbsp (30 mL) flour
1/4 cup (60 mL) water

● ● ● ○

Combine all ingredients, except flour and water, in a slow cooker. Cover and cook on low heat for 8 to 9 hours, or until vegetables and beef are tender.

Mix flour and water; slowly add to beef mixture. Cover and cook on high heat setting for 10 to 15 minutes, or until thickened. Remove bay leaves and serve.

● ● ● ○

SERVES 6

Recipe by Brandon Boone

Photography: Brian Gould

Pair With:
• Chateauneuf-Du-Pape
• Australian Shiraz
• Stout Beer

Balsamic Marinated Bison Sirloin with Wild Mushroom Hunter Sauce

1/2 cup (125 mL) balsamic vinegar
1 tbsp (15 mL) soy sauce
1 tbsp (15 mL) tomato paste
freshly cracked black pepper
4, 4 oz (125 g) bison sirloin steaks
8 oz (250 g) chopped fresh wild mushrooms OR rehydrated dry mushrooms
1 tbsp (15 mL) butter
1/4 cup (60 mL) dry white wine
1 cup (250 mL) beef, veal OR bison stock
1 Roma tomato, peeled, seeded and diced
1 tbsp (15 mL) whipping cream
salt and pepper to taste

● ● ● ○

Combine vinegar, soy, tomato paste and pepper. Toss bison in marinade. Marinate in refrigerator for 4 hours.

Preheat oven to 200°F (93°C).

Heat a skillet over medium-high heat. Remove bison from marinade; rinsing off and patting dry. Place 1 bison steak in skillet. Sear on one side for 1 minute, flip and sear second side for the same amount of time. Transfer bison to oven to keep warm. Repeat with remaining steaks. Add mushrooms to skillet with butter; sauté until soft. Add wine and let reduce. Add stock and reduce by half. Stir in tomato and cream; season with salt and pepper.

Cut each bison steak into thin strips. On each of 4 plates, fan out slices. Spoon Hunter Sauce around steak and serve immediately.

● ● ● ○

SERVES 4

Recipe by chef Alex Svenne
Photography: Brian Gould

Pair With:
• Washington State Syrah
• Chateauneuf du Pape
• Super Tuscan

Oak Smoked Elk Rib-eye

Oak wood is an excellent alternative to mesquite and hickory, especially when cooking red meat such as elk.

1 cup (250 mL) brown sugar
1/2 cup (125 mL) minced garlic
1 tsp (5 mL) dried chile flakes
1 tbsp (15 mL) EACH, paprika and
    coarse salt
1 tsp (5 mL) freshly ground black
    poppor
1/4 cup (60 mL) balsamic vinegar

2.2 lb (1 kg) elk rib-eye roast OR
    beef, bison or other game roast
2 cups (500 mL) oak wood chips

● ● ● ○

In a bowl, combine sugar, garlic and spices; add enough balsamic vinegar to make a paste. Spread over roast. Cover, refrigerate and marinate overnight or up to 2 days.

Insert a thermometer into the roast and prepare smoker following the manufacturer's directions. Once coals have turned grey, place elk roast on first rack of smoker and cover. Place 1 cup (250 mL) of oak chips on top of coals and close smoker door. Once smoke has subsided, add remaining wood chips to smoker. Continue to cook elk roast until internal temperature reaches 120°F to 140°F (50°C to 60°C) or more, depending on the degree of doneness preferred. Cooking time should be approximately 1 1/2 to 2 hours, but outside conditions will play a factor in the length of time needed to reach the desired internal temperature.

● ● ● ○

SERVES 6-8

Recipe by chef Alex Svenne

Photography: Brian Gould

Pair With:
• Canadian Baco Noir
• Washington Shiraz
• Organic Merlot

DESSERTS
& Sweets

Dried Vanilla Bean, Strawberry, Peach, Pineapple & Banana Shish Kebabs

4 vanilla beans, seeds removed
seeds from vanilla beans
3 tbsp (45 mL) orange brandy
6 large strawberries, hulled and cut in half
2 ripe peaches, pitted and cut into bite-sized pieces
1/2 ripe pineapple, peeled, cored and cut into bite-sized pieces
2 large, just ripe bananas, peeled and cut into bite-sized pieces
2 tbsp (30 mL) butter, melted
3 tbsp (45 mL) light brown sugar

● ● ● ●

Preheat oven to 300°F (150°C). Split vanilla beans in half and remove seeds, reserving. Place vanilla beans in oven and bake until firm. Remove from oven and let cool.

In a large bowl, combine reserved vanilla bean seeds, brandy and fruit. Mix well, making sure to coat all fruit. Remove fruit from marinade and thread onto vanilla bean skewers. Preheat a gas grill. Place skewers on barbecue and grill for about 3 to 4 minutes a side. Just before removing from grill, brush with melted butter and dust with brown sugar. Serve immediately.

● ● ● ●

Recipe by Brandon Boone

Photography: Brian Gould

Pair With:
• B.C. Late Harvest Optima
• Chilean Late Harvest Sauvignon Blanc
• Ontario Vidal Icewine

Ⓜ angoes Foster-Style

2 large mangoes
1/4 cup (60 mL) butter, melted
1 cup (250 mL) Demerara sugar
2 tbsp (30 mL) XO Original Canadian Maple Syrup Liqueur
1/4 cup (60 mL) dark rum
pinch EACH, cinnamon AND ground nutmeg (reserve some nutmeg for dusting)
dollop of light sour cream OR yogurt

● ● ● ●

Cube mangoes and place in a square aluminum-foil pan. In a separate bowl, combine butter, sugar, liqueur, rum, cinnamon and nutmeg. Pour over mangoes and toss. Seal foil pan with aluminum foil. Place on medium-hot area of fire pit grill for 8 to 10 minutes. Remove from fire. Open pan carefully. Spoon mangoes into individual serving dishes. Top with sour cream. Dust with more nutmeg.

● ● ● ●

SERVES 4 TO 6

Recipe by Shel Zolkewich
Photography: Brian Gould

Pair With:
• Banrock Station Sparkling Chardonnay
• Fonseca Bin 27 Fine reserve Port

Double-Berry Crêpes with Vanilla Whipped Cream

Crêpes:
1 cup (250 mL) instant pancake mix
3/4 cup (175 mL) water

Fruit Topping:
1/4 cup (60 mL) EACH, raspberries and blueberries, fresh or frozen
1 tbsp (15 mL) sugar
fresh lemon juice

Vanilla Whipped Cream Filling:
1/2 cup (125 mL) whipping cream
4 oz (125 g) cream cheese, softened
1 tsp (5 mL) vanilla extract
1 tbsp (15 mL) lemon juice

● ● ● ●

Crêpes: Combine pancake mix and water. Heat a crêpe pan or non-stick skillet and pour in 1/2 cup (125 mL) of batter; swirl to coat entire pan. Cook crêpes until golden brown on both sides. Repeat to use up all of the batter.

Topping: In a saucepan, heat berries, sugar and lemon juice over low heat until thickened.

Filling: Beat cream, cream cheese, vanilla and lemon juice until well mixed.

Place a line of filling in the centre of each crêpe and roll. Pour fruit topping over crêpes and serve immediately.

● ● ● ●

SERVES 2

Recipe by Julian Scott & Colin Gandier
Photography: Brian Gould

Blushing Poached Pears in Cinnamon Vanilla Syrup

3/4 cup (175 mL) sugar
1 tsp (5 mL) vanilla extract
1 cinnamon stick
1 cup (250 mL) water
1 cup (250 mL) Western Premium Light beer
8 Anjou OR Bartlett pears
2 tbsp (30 mL) lime juice
4 cups (1 L) fresh raspberries OR 2, 10 oz (285 g) pkgs frozen raspberries

● ● ● ●

In a large skillet, simmer sugar, vanilla, cinnamon stick, water and beer for 5 minutes. Peel pears leaving their stems attached. Coat with lime juice to prevent browning. Poach pears over low heat in sugar syrup, turning often. When pears are tender, remove with a slotted spoon to a shallow rimmed dish. Set aside.

Bring remaining syrup to a boil. Continue to boil until reduced to 1 cup (250 mL); remove cinnamon stick and discard. Add lime juice and raspberries to syrup and cook until sauce turns red, about 5 minutes. Strain and pour over pears. Cover pears and refrigerate until cold, turning frequently to coat. Place poached pears on individual dessert plates. Garnish with a spoonful of sauce and a dollop of whipped cream.

● ● ● ●

SERVES 6

Recipe courtesy of
   Great Western Brewery
Photography: Brian Gould

Maple Pots de Crème

A uniquely Canadian dessert – smooth and seductive.

1 1/4 cups (300 mL) maple syrup
1 1/4 cups (300 mL) whipping cream
1/4 cup (60 mL) cornstarch
1/4 cup (60 mL) cold water
1/2 tsp (2 mL) vanilla extract

● ● ● ●

Stir syrup with cream in a small saucepan. Mix cornstarch with cold water; stir into syrup mixture. Cook over medium heat, stirring frequently, especially as the mixture becomes hot and begins to bubble. Let bubble for 1 1/2 to 2 minutes, or until thickened.

Remove from heat, stir in vanilla and pour into small cups suitable for serving.

Refrigerate until set; then cover until ready to serve (within 2 days).

● ● ● ●

MAKES 8 SERVINGS

Recipe by Marilyn Bentz Crowley

Chilled Amaretto Zabaglione

4 egg yolks
1/4 cup (60 mL) amaretto
   liqueur
3 tbsp (45 mL) superfine sugar
1 cup (250 mL) whipping
   cream
crushed amaretti cookies for
   garnish

• • • •

Combine yolks, amaretto and sugar in a heatproof bowl and whisk until well blended. Fill a saucepan with water and bring to a simmer, not a boil. Place bowl over simmering water and continue to whisk until yolk mixture becomes light and fluffy, about 5 minutes. Remove from heat and reserve.

In a separate bowl, whip cream until fluffy then add to the egg mixture, folding in gently. Pour into champagne flutes and chill for a couple of hours. Before serving, garnish with crushed cookies.

• • • •

SERVES 4

Recipe by Brandon Boone
Photography: Brian Gould

Pair With:
• Italian Brachetto
• French Muscat de Beaumes de Venice
• B.C. Vidal Icewine

Individual Tiramisù

2 egg yolks
1 cup (250 mL) mascarpone cheese
1/4 cup (60 mL) light brown sugar
1 cup (250 mL) whipping cream
1/2 cup (125 mL) brewed espresso coffee
2 tbsp (30 mL) dark rum
24 ladyfinger cookies
1/2 cup (125 mL) chopped dark Belgian chocolate

● ● ● ●

In a bowl, combine yolks, cheese and brown sugar; whisk until mixture is well blended. Fold in whipped cream; set aside.

In a shallow pan, combine coffee and rum; break ladyfingers in half and, one at a time, dunk into coffee mixture very briefly, turning over once. Divide dunked ladyfingers among 4 martini glasses. Layer each with mascarpone cheese mixture and chopped chocolate. Repeat process until glass is filled and last ingredient is chopped chocolate. Cover and refrigerate overnight to chill.

● ● ● ●

SERVES 4

Recipe by Brandon Boone
Photography: Brian Gould

Pair With:
• Italian Moscato d'Asti
• Chilean Late Harvest Sauvignon Blanc
• Pineau des Charentes

Grand Marnier Chocolate Mousse with Saskatoon Berries

1 cup (250 mL) whipping
  cream
8 oz (250 g) dark chocolate
  chunks
4 large eggs, separated
1/2 tsp (2 mL) vanilla extract
1/4 cup (60 mL) icing
  (confectioner's) sugar
2 oz (60 mL) Grand Marnier
1/2 cup (125 mL) raspberry
  yogurt
2 tbsp (30 mL) Saskatoon
  berry jam
4 chocolate cups
4 chocolate leaves OR curls
fresh mint leaves for garnish

• • • •

With an electric mixer, beat cream until stiff peaks form. Set aside.

Fill a medium-sized pot with water and bring to a boil; reduce heat to medium. Add chocolate chunks to a bowl large enough to rest on the rim of the pot; melt chocolate over hot water, stirring constantly until smooth (or microwave at half power for 1 1/2 minute intervals, stirring in between, until melted). Whisk in egg yolks and vanilla; mix well and transfer to a large bowl.

Beat egg whites in a separate bowl while gradually adding icing sugar; continue to beat until stiff peaks form. Gently fold beaten whites into chocolate mixture, first incorporating a small amount of whites into the chocolate mixture to temper it, then fold in the rest of the whites. Fold in whipped cream and 1 oz (30 mL) of Grand Marnier. Turn into individual chocolate cups. Chill before serving.

To Assemble: Spoon 1/4 cup (60 mL) raspberry yogurt onto 4 dessert plates. Place 1 tsp (5 mL) of the Saskatoon berry jam in the centre of the yogurt. Using a toothpick, pull the jam from the centre out to make a design in the yogurt. Fill chocolate cups with mousse and place on top of yogurt; drizzle each with 1/2 tsp (2 mL) Grand Marnier. Garnish with chocolate leaves and mint sprigs.

• • • •

SERVES 4

Recipe by Julian Scott & Andrew Gandier
Photography: Brian Gould

$\textcircled{R}$ hubarb & Ginger Crumble

Crumble Topping:
1/2 cup (125 mL) whole-wheat flour
1/3 cup plus 1 tbsp (90 mL) butter
1/2 cup (125 mL) oatmeal
1/2 cup (125 mL) brown sugar

2 lbs (1 kg) rhubarb cut into 1" (2.5 cm) chunks
1/3 cup (75 mL) plus 1 tbsp (15 mL) brown sugar
1 tsp (5 mL) powdered ginger

● ● ● ●

Topping: Place flour in a large mixing bowl; add butter and, using fingertips, rub lightly into flour; add oatmeal and brown sugar and combine well with flour mixture.

Preheat oven to 350°F (180°C). In a saucepan over low heat, combine rhubarb, sugar and ginger. Cook, covered, for 15 minutes, stirring often (don't overcook; it should be chunky, not mushy). When done, drain off half the liquid in the pan, then transfer the mixture to a pie plate. Sprinkle with crumble topping and bake 30 to 40 minutes, or until topping has browned.

● ● ● ●

SERVES 8

Recipe by
  Ali Ward-Flanagan
Photography:
  John Ulan/Epic Photography

any Berries Crumble

This dessert is a perfect finale to a roasted pork meal.

3 cups (750 mL) mixed fresh berries (blueberries, raspberries, strawberries,
  blackberries)
1 cup (250 mL) large-flake quick oatmeal
1/2 cup (125 mL) flour
3/4 cup (175 mL) Demerara sugar
1/2 tsp (2 mL) cinnamon
1/2 cup (125 mL) butter, melted
1/4 tsp (1 mL) freshly ground nutmeg

● ● ● ●

Place fruit in a shallow casserole. Combine oatmeal, flour, sugar and cinnamon in a
small bowl. Pour in melted butter and mix until a loose crumble forms. Spread crumble evenly over fruit. Bake at 350°F (180°C) for 40 minutes. Remove and dust with
nutmeg.

● ● ● ●

SERVES 8

Recipe by Shel Zolkewich
Photography: Brian Gould

Profiterole Swans with Lemon Sorbet on a Pond of Honeydew Mint Jus

Swans:
1/2 cup (125 mL) milk OR water
2 tbsp (30 mL) butter
1/2 cup (125 mL) flour
pinch of salt
2 eggs

1 cup (250 mL) lemon gelato

Honeydew Mint Jus:
1 cup (250 mL) diced honeydew
1 tbsp (15 mL) chopped fresh mint

● ● ● ●

Swans: In a saucepan over medium-high heat, bring milk and butter to a boil. Reduce heat to medium. Add flour and salt and mix vigorously until it forms a thick paste. Remove from heat and let cool for 2 minutes. Using an electric stand mixer (or hand-held), add 1 egg to flour mixture and beat until absorbed. Add second egg and beat until dough no longer looks glossy.

Preheat oven to 400°F (200°C). Grease 2 small cookie sheets. Using a piping bag with a star tip, pipe 4, 2" (5 cm) ovals (make a few extra, just in case). On second sheet with a small round tip, pipe 4 swan neck shapes. Squeeze a little harder on piping bag at head end of neck to make head shape (definitely do a few extra).

Put both pans in oven and bake for 5 minutes. Remove only the necks from oven. Reduce oven temperature to 325°F (160°F) and bake for 20 to 25 minutes, or until golden coloured. Remove from oven and poke with a paring knife to let steam out. Cool completely. Cut profiteroles in half, lengthwise. Cut top piece in half lengthwise.

Jus: In a blender, purée melon and mint until smooth. If melon is a little hard or underripe add 1 tsp (5 mL) of honey to sweeten.

To Assemble: Spoon a small scoop of sorbet into each profiterole bottom. Prop wings next to sorbet. Prop neck up in front of sorbet (swans can now be frozen until ready to serve). Place a Profiterole Swan in the centre of each of 4 chilled plates or shallow soup plates. Spoon Honeydew Mint Jus around swans.

● ● ● ●

SERVES 4

Recipe by chef Alex Svenne
Photography: Brian Gould

Pair With:
• Champagne
• German Auslese Riesling
• Late Harvest Semillon

maretto Snowballs

1 cup (250 mL) unsalted butter
1/2 cup (125 mL) icing (confectioner's) sugar
2 1/2 cups (625 mL) all-purpose flour
1 tsp (5 mL) salt
2 tbsp (30 mL) Amaretto liqueur
icing (confectioner's) sugar, for rolling

Glaze:
3 tbsp (45 mL) icing (confectioner's) sugar
1/4 cup (60 mL) Amaretto

almonds, slivered or sliced, for decorating (optional)

● ● ● ●

Preheat oven to 350°F (180°C).

Cream butter and sugar in a large mixing bowl. Add flour and salt and mix until blended. Add amaretto. Roll dough into small balls using icing sugar to keep dough from sticking. Place on parchment-lined cookie sheet approximately 1" (2.5 cm) apart. Bake for 8 to 10 minutes. Remove from oven and let cool on a wire rack. Dip cookies in glaze made by mixing icing sugar with Amaretto. Top cookies with slivered almonds.

● ● ● ●

MAKES APPROXIMATELY 24 TO 36 COOKIES

Recipe by Claudine Gervais
Photography: Brian Gould

anilla Cognac Stars

1 cup (250 mL) unsalted butter
1 cup (250 mL) sugar
2 eggs
1/4 cup (60 mL) vanilla cognac, (such as Navan)
2 cups (500 mL) flour
2 tsp (10 mL) cream of tartar
1 tsp (5 mL) baking soda
1 tsp (5 mL) salt

● ● ● ●

Cream butter and sugar in a large mixing bowl. Add eggs, 1 at a time, until blended. Add cognac and blend until incorporated.

In another bowl, combine dry ingredients. Add to batter a little at a time, mixing until blended. Divide dough in half, form into balls and flatten into a disc shape. Wrap in plastic wrap and refrigerate overnight.

Preheat oven to 350°F (180°C). Roll out dough on a floured surface, dusting with flour if dough is sticking to surface or rolling pin. Roll dough to approximately 1/4" (6 mm) thickness. Using a star cookie cutter, cut dough into stars. Place 2" (5 cm) apart on a parchment-lined baking sheet. Bake until edges start to lightly brown, approximately 8 minutes, depending on size of cookie cutter used. Remove from oven and let cool on a wire rack.

● ● ● ●

MAKES APPROXIMATELY 36 COOKIES

Recipe by Claudine Gervais
Photography: Brian Gould

Dried Cherry, Grand Marnier & Almond Biscotti

Soft and chewy deep red cherries add a festive jewel-tone to these crisp buttery biscotti.

1 small orange
4 cups (1 L) all-purpose flour
1 1/2 tsp (7 mL) baking powder
1/2 tsp (2 mL) salt
1 1/2 cups (375 mL) sliced or
   coarsely chopped almonds, divided
4 large eggs
1 1/3 cups (325 mL) granulated
   sugar
1/3 cup (75 mL) butter, melted
1 tbsp (15 mL) Grand Marnier
1 tsp (5 mL) vanilla extract
1 cup (250 mL) dried cherries

• • • •

Preheat oven to 325°F (160°C). Line a large baking sheet with aluminum foil or parchment paper. Grate orange zest into long thin strips with a zesting tool or microplane; reserve. Stir flour with baking powder, salt, zest and 1 cup (250 mL) almonds.

Using an electric mixer, beat eggs until fluffy and light coloured. Slowly beat in sugar, then butter, Grand Marnier and vanilla. Pour into flour mixture; stir until dry mixture is almost absorbed. Then stir in dried cherries until well combined.

With moistened hands, divide dough in half; form each half into a loaf about 15" (38 cm) long and 4" (10 cm) wide on lined baking sheet. Loaves should be at least 2" (5 cm) apart. Scatter remaining almonds evenly over tops; lightly press into dough. Bake 35 to 40 minutes, or until small cracks are visible and tops are golden. Slide hot loaves onto a large cutting board; cut crosswise into 1/2" (1.3 cm) thick slices. Stand slices upright about 1/2" (1.3 cm) apart on baking sheet.

Reduce oven temperature to 300°F (150°C). Bake 30 to 35 minutes, or until biscotti are dry to the touch. Cool on a baking sheet placed on a rack; store in an airtight container for several days or freeze for weeks.

• • • •

MAKES 48 BISCOTTI

Recipe by Marilyn Bentz Crowley
Photography: Brian Gould

Pair With
• Grand Marnier
• Vidal Icewine

Chocolate Kahlúa & Pecan Cookies

1 cup (250 mL) unsalted butter
2 cups (500 mL) brown sugar
2 eggs
1/4 cup (60 mL) Kahlúa liqueur
2 1/2 cups (625 mL) all-purpose flour
1 tsp (5 mL) salt
1 tsp (5 mL) baking soda
1/4 cup (60 mL) unsweetened cocoa
1 cup (250 mL) chopped pecans
1 1/2 cups (375 mL) chocolate chips (semi-sweet OR milk chocolate)

● ○ ● ○

Preheat oven to 375°F (190°C). In an electric stand mixer bowl, combine butter and sugar; cream together on high speed. Add eggs, 1 at a time, until incorporated. Add Kahlúa; beat until smooth. In a separate bowl, combine flour, salt, baking soda and cocoa. Add to butter mixture and mix to incorporate. Stir in nuts and chocolate chips. Drop dough by tablespoonfuls onto a parchment-lined baking sheet, leaving approximately 2" (5 cm) between cookies. Bake for 8 to 10 minutes, or until the edges are lightly browned. Place on wire racks to cool.

● ○ ● ○

MAKES APPROXIMATELY 36 COOKIES

Recipe by Claudine Gervais
Photography: Brian Gould

ⒷRandy Coronets with Maple Mousse & Raspberries

Brandy Coronets:
1/2 cup (125 mL) maple syrup
1/4 cup (60 mL) butter
1/2 cup (125 mL) flour
pinch of salt
2 tsp (10 mL) brandy

Maple Mousse:
2 egg whites
1/4 cup (60 mL) maple syrup
1 cup (250 mL) whipping cream

8 large raspberries
8 mint leaves

• • • •

Coronets: Preheat oven to 350°F (180°C). In a saucepan over medium-high heat, combine syrup and butter; bring to a boil. Add flour, salt and brandy, stirring until it forms a paste. Line a baking sheet with parchment paper (or a Silpat). Drop 4 teaspoonfuls of dough onto parchment-lined sheets. Bake for 7 minutes, or until the edges are golden brown. Remove from oven and, while still warm, wrap each wafer around a metal cone-shaped mould. Coronets will harden as they cool.

Mousse: Using an electric mixer, beat egg whites until stiff. Slowly add maple syrup while mixing. In a separate bowl, beat cream until stiff. Fold egg whites into whipped cream.

Pipe mousse into coronets and top each with 1 raspberry and 1 mint leaf; serve immediately.

• • • •

SERVES 4

Recipe by chef Alex Svenne
Photography: Brian Gould

Pair With:
• Cava
• Pineau des Charentes

Cinnamon-Hazelnut Torte with Cinnamon Cream

Crisp Wafers and luscious Cinnamon Cream are combined in this delectable torte. It is suitable for a dairy-based Passover meal.

Cinnamon-Hazelnut Torte:

6 egg whites
1 1/2 cups (375 mL) granulated sugar
3/4 cup (175 mL) sifted matzo cake meal
3/4 cup (175 mL) whole toasted hazelnuts (filberts), husks removed and nuts
   finely ground
3/4 cup (175 mL) unsalted butter, melted
2 tbsp (30 mL) water
1 tbsp (15 mL) vanilla extract

Cinnamon-Hazelnut Torte
(continued)

Cinnamon Cream:
3 cups (750 mL) whipping cream
1/4 cup (60 mL) berry sugar OR extra-fine granulated sugar
2 tsp (10 mL) ground cinnamon
3/4 cup (175 mL) whole toasted hazelnuts (filberts), husks removed and nuts
  coarsely chopped

● ◦ ● ◦

Torte: In a large bowl, lightly whisk egg whites by hand until foamy. Gradually whisk in sugar, then matzo meal and finely ground hazelnuts. Whisk in butter, water and vanilla. Let stand for 10 minutes. Draw 8" (25 cm) circles on parchment paper; drop 1/3 cup (75 mL) of batter onto each circle. Using a metal spatula, spread batter evenly to edges of circle. Transfer to baking sheets and bake in upper third of 400°F (200°C) oven for 9 to 10 minutes, or until lightly browned.

Remove torte wafer, along with parchment paper, to cooling rack. Let rest for several minutes. Remove baked torte wafer and set on rack to cool completely. Continue with batter until you have 12 wafers. Torte wafers can be made several days in advance and stored between sheets of waxed paper in an airtight container.

Cream: In a chilled metal bowl, whip cream with berry sugar until soft peaks form. Add cinnamon. Beat to stiff peaks. Spread 1 tbsp (15 mL) of cinnamon cream on a serving plate. Set 1 layer on top, pressing down to secure layer in place. Cover torte layer with 1/2 cup (125 mL) of cinnamon cream, spreading cream to the very edge of the layer; sprinkle with 1 tbsp (15 mL) chopped hazelnuts. Cover with next torte layer, pressing down gently to adhere. Continue spreading cream and sprinkling nuts with remaining layers. Garnish top of cake with cinnamon cream and chopped hazelnuts. Refrigerate for several hours prior to serving. This will make enough for a very light cream layer between each wafer. Double the recipe if you would like more filling.

● ◦ ● ◦

SERVES 8 TO 12

Recipe by CJ Katz
Photography: Brian Gould

D ark Chocolate Snare Drum with Hazelnut Tuille Drumsticks

Snare Drum:
1 cup (250 mL) whipping cream
12 oz (340 g) bittersweet chocolate, chopped
1 tsp (5 mL) vanilla
2 oz (55 g) white chocolate, chopped

Hazelnut Tuille Drumsticks:
1/2 cup (125 mL) finely ground hazelnuts
1/4 cup (60 mL) flour
1/2 cup (125 mL) sugar
1/4 tsp (1 mL) salt
2 large egg whites
1/3 cup (75 mL) butter, melted

• • • •

Drum: In a saucepan set over medium-high heat, bring cream to a boil; pour cream into a heat-proof bowl filled with bittersweet chocolate. Let sit 1 minute then mix until smooth. Stir in vanilla. Pour into 4, 3" (7.5 cm) ramekins. Refrigerate for 2 hours, or until set.

Unmould ramekins by partially submerging in warm water. Invert and drop chocolate drums onto a sheet of parchment. In a heatproof bowl, microwave white chocolate until melted. Transfer to a piping bag fitted with a small round tip. Pipe a criss-cross pattern all around the outside of the chocolate drums. Pipe a band around the entire base and top of drums.

Drumsticks: Preheat oven to 325°F (160°C). Line a baking sheet with parchment paper. In a bowl, combine hazelnuts, flour, sugar and salt; whisk to mix. Whisk in egg whites and butter until combined. Pipe 8, 6" (15 cm) long strips onto parchment paper. Bake in oven for 5 minutes, or until golden. Using a thin spatula, remove cookies 1 at a time from baking sheet. Twist cookies around a wooden spoon handle, making sure to work quickly. Cool cookies completely.

Place 1 drum in the centre of each of 4 plates. Top with 2 drumsticks each and serve immediately.

• • • •

SERVES 4

Recipe by Alex Svenne
Photography: Brian Gould

Pair With:
• Champagne
• Ruby Port
• Sparkling Shiraz

Chocolate Lava Pots

Caramel Sauce:
1 cup (250 mL) unsalted butter
2 cups (500 mL) whipping cream
1/4 cup (60 mL) granulated sugar
1 cup (250 mL) brown sugar
2 tbsp (30 mL) vanilla extract
2 cups (500 mL) corn syrup
1/2 tsp (2 mL) salt

Lava Pots:
1 recipe of Caramel Sauce (see above)
1/4 cup (60 mL) granulated sugar
1/2 cup (125 mL) brewed coffee
1 cup (250 mL) unsalted butter
1 cup (250 mL) chopped unsweetened Baker's chocolate
4 eggs
1 oz. (30 mL) Frangelico liqueur

● ● ● ●

Sauce: In a heavy-bottomed saucepan, combine butter, 1 cup (250 mL) cream, sugars, vanilla, syrup and salt. Bring to a boil. Boil for 20 to 30 minutes. Once thick slow bubbles start to appear, remove from heat and add 1 cup (250 mL) cold cream. Let cool completely.

Lava Pots: Preheat oven to 325°F (160°C). Into each of 8, 1/2 cup (125 mL) ungreased ramekins spoon 2 heaping tbsp (40 mL) cold caramel sauce. Set aside. In a saucepan, combine sugar, coffee and butter. Bring to a boil; turn off heat and add chocolate, stirring until it melts. Let sit for 5 minutes, then whisk in eggs and liqueur. Pour chocolate mixture over caramel sauce, filling ramekins to the top. Bake in a water bath for 30 to 45 minutes. Serve warm in ramekins with vanilla ice cream, whipping cream and chocolate-covered gooseberries.

● ● ● ●

MAKES 8

Recipe by chef Adam Sperling

Pair with:
• Mission Hill Vidal Icewine
• Essensia 2000
• Dienhard Beeren Auslese

aris by Midnight

A sublime dessert from chef Fuller's time at the Paris Ritz Hotel.

Chocolate Sponge:
1 cup (250 mL) sugar
1 cup (250 mL) eggs
1 tsp (5 mL) vanilla
1 cup (250 mL) flour
4 tsp (20 mL) cocoa powder, sifted

Chocolate Mousse:
1 1/4 cups (300 mL) whipping cream
3 large egg yolks
1/2 cup (125 mL) sugar
2 tbsp (30 mL) water
8 oz (250 g) bittersweet chocolate
2 tbsp (30 mL) unsalted butter

● ● ● ●

Sponge: Preheat oven to 350°F (180°C). Beat sugar with eggs and vanilla. Fold in flour. Add sifted cocoa powder. Pour batter into a tube pan and bake for 30 minutes. Remove and place on rack to cool.

Mousse: In a bowl, whip cream until soft peaks form. In a separate bowl, whisk yolks until thick, approximately 2 minutes. In a saucepan over medium-high heat, combine sugar and water; bring to a boil for 1 minute. Pour sugar mixture over yolks and beat again. In a bowl set over a saucepan of simmering water (the water should not touch the bottom of the bowl), melt chocolate and butter, stirring occasionally. Remove bowl from heat and let cool until just warm. Fold egg mixture and whipped cream into chocolate mixture until combined. Refrigerate mousse for approximately 2 hours, or until set.

To Assemble: Split cake in half. Make a tunnel in bottom half by removing pieces of cake, leaving a 1/4" (6 mm) border. Reserve cake pieces for another use. Fill tunnel with chocolate mousse. Garnish with cocoa powder or icing (confectioner's) sugar, orange segments or fresh mint leaves.

● ● ● ●

Recipe by chef Rob Fuller
Photography: Patricia Holdsworth

Grilled Maple-Glazed Angel Food Cake with Saskatoon Topping & Whipped Cream

1 angel food cake
3/4 cup (175 mL) maple syrup
1/2 tsp (2 mL) freshly ground nutmeg
saskatoon berry fruit topping OR blueberry topping
whipped cream

● ● ● ●

Cut cake into 12 portions. Brush both sides of each slice with maple syrup. Place slices on a clean preheated grill over medium heat. When grill marks appear, turn and grill the other side. Remove from heat and dust with fresh nutmeg. Top with saskatoon topping and whipped cream.

● ● ● ●

MAKES 12 SERVINGS

Recipe by Shel Zolkewich
Photography: Brian Gould

Shortbread Squares with Cranberry & Walnut Topping

Cranberry Relish:
2 cups (500 mL) cranberries, fresh or frozen
grated zest of 1 orange
1 small orange, peeled and seeded
3/4 cup (175 mL) sugar

Shortbread:
2 cups (500 mL) flour
1/2 cup (125 mL) sugar
pinch of salt
3/4 cup (175 mL) butter, softened

Topping:
3 cups (750 mL) Cranberry Relish
1 cup (250 mL) chopped walnuts
2 eggs
3 tbsp (45 mL) flour

● ● ● ●

Relish: In a food processor, combine cranberries, zest, orange and sugar; process until roughly chopped.

Shortbread: Preheat oven to 350°F (180°C). In a large bowl, combine flour, sugar and salt; add butter and mix with a pastry blender or hands until mixture forms small crumbs. Press into the bottom of a 9 x 13" (23 x 33 cm) baking pan. Bake for approximately 25 minutes. Remove from oven and let cool.

Topping: In a large bowl, combine Cranberry Relish, walnuts, eggs and flour; mix thoroughly. Spread topping evenly over baked crust. Return to oven and bake for 30 to 35 minutes. Remove from oven and let cool before serving.

● ● ● ●

MAKES 12 SQUARES OR 48 DAINTIES

Recipe by chef Beth Traynor
Photography: Patricia Holdsworth

Okanagan Apple Tarte Tatin with Maple Syrup Ice Cream

If you can, make the ice cream from scratch; if you can't, purchased ice cream will do in a pinch.

1/2 cup (125 mL) sugar
4 Okanagan apples, Gala type OR
   Golden Delicious, peeled cored and
   quartered
1/2 a vanilla bean
1/4 cup (60 mL) butter
2 tbsp (30 mL) raisins soaked in rum
6 disks puff pastry
1 egg beaten with 1 tbsp (15 mL) water

Maple Syrup Ice Cream:
1 cup (250 mL) homogenized milk
1 cup (250 mL) whipping cream
4 egg yolks
3/4 cup (175 mL) maple syrup

• • • •

Heat a heavy-bottomed saucepan over medium heat until pan is warmed; add sugar. Let sugar sit until you can see it start to melt. At that point, give pan a good shake and let sugar cook some more. Once it has melted even further, stir with a wooden spoon. Continue cooking and stirring until sugar turns into liquid. Add 2 tbsp (30 mL) hot water to pan, making sure to protect hands as liquid will sputter. Stir to mix; if any lumps have formed, return to heat and stir until they dissolve. Add apples and cook in the caramel with vanilla bean. Once apples are soft, stir in butter; add raisins and mix well. Spoon out some of the apples and raisins into each of 6 ramekins, with a little caramel sauce as well. On top of each, place a disk of puff pastry (like a seal); brush with egg wash and then bake in a water bath at 375°F (190°C) for about 35 minutes.

Ice Cream: In a saucepan over medium-low heat, combine and warm milk and cream. In a heatproof bowl, mix yolks with maple syrup, then slowly add warm milk mixture to egg mixture to temper it. Place bowl over a gently simmering pot of water and whisk until thickened to a custard consistency. Remove from heat and chill until cool. Place cream mixture in an ice-cream maker and follow manufacturer's instructions to make ice cream.

Place 1 tart upside down on each of 4 serving plates. Dust with icing sugar and top with Maple Syrup Ice Cream, which will melt and form a nice sauce.

* Place ramekins in a baking pan large enough to hold all 6 and able to hold about 2" (5 cm) water.

• • • •

SERVES 4

Recipe by chef Guiseppe Posteraro
Photography: Hamid Attie Photography

Pair With:
• Italian Asti Spumante
• B.C. Late Harvest Optima
• French Sauternes

Dessert Club Sandwich with Pineapple Fries & Strawberry Ketchup

Chocolate Pound Cake:
2 cups (500 mL) all-purpose flour
1 cup (250 mL) cocoa powder
1 tsp (5 mL) baking powder
1/2 tsp (2 mL) baking soda
1/2 tsp (2 mL) salt
1 1/2 cups (375 mL) butter (room temperature)
2 3/4 cups (675 mL) sugar
2 tsp (10 mL) vanilla
2 tsp (10 mL) coffee extract (optional)
5 eggs
1 1/4 cups (300 mL) buttermilk

Whipped Cream:
1 tbsp (15 mL) sugar
1 tsp (5 mL) vanilla extract
1 cup (250 mL) whipping cream

White Chocolate Slice:
1 oz (30 g) white chocolate, chopped
2 tbsp (30 mL) whipping cream

Strawberry Ketchup:
2 cups (500 g) ripe strawberries, cored
1/4 cup (60 mL) water
3 tbsp (45 mL) sugar
2 tsp (10 mL) fresh lemon juice

Pineapple Fries:
1 fresh pineapple, peeled and trimmed into a square
1/2 cup (125 mL) light brown sugar
1/4 cup (60 mL) unsalted butter

4 large ripe strawberries, cored and cut into 1/4" (6 mm) slices
8 large fresh basil leaves (4 per layer)
1 ripe banana cut lengthwise into 1/2" (1.3 cm) strips

Dessert Club Sandwich
(continued)

● ○ ● ○

Cake: Preheat oven to 325°F (160°C). Grease 2, 9 x 5" (23 x 12 cm) loaf pans with butter. Dust well with sugar. Sift together flour, cocoa, baking powder, baking soda and salt. Set aside. Using an electric mixer, cream butter on medium speed until fluffy. Add sugar, vanilla and coffee extract; beat until light and fluffy, about 3 to 5 minutes. Scrape down bowl halfway through mixing. Beating at medium speed, add eggs 1 at a time; beat until well blended before adding next egg. Reduce speed to low and add flour mixture in parts, alternating with buttermilk, about 3 times each. Batter should be smooth. Pour batter into prepared pans and bake 50 to 60 minutes, until top feels springy and a toothpick inserted into the centre comes out clean. Cool loaves in pans on wire racks for 20 minutes. Turn out loaves onto wire racks to finish cooling. Cut end off 1 side of 1 cake. Slice 3, 3/4" (2 cm) pieces of cake. Freeze remaining cake for another occasion.

Cream: Combine sugar, vanilla and cream in the bowl of an electric mixer. Beat on high until soft peaks form. Cover and chill.

White Chocolate: Place chocolate in a heatproof bowl and microwave until melted. Add cream and whisk to incorporate. On a piece of waxed paper, draw a 4" (10 cm) square. Turn waxed paper over so pencil line is on the other side. Place waxed paper on a flat plate and pour just enough chocolate onto waxed paper to fill square, using a spatula to clean-up edges. Let cool to room temperature.

Strawberry Ketchup: Place strawberries, water, sugar and lemon juice in a blender; purée until smooth. Cover and chill.

Fries: Cut pineapple into several 1/2" (1.3 cm) squares. Using a crinkle-cut knife, cut 16, 2 x 1/2 x 1/2" (5 x 1.3 x 1.3 cm) pineapple "fries," avoiding the core. Roll in brown sugar and set aside. Melt butter in a skillet over medium-high heat; add pineapple and caramelize on all sides, turning frequently. Remove from pan and let rest on paper towels to absorb any excess butter.

To Assemble: Spread a layer of whipped cream on 1 piece of cake; top with an even layer of basil, the White Chocolate Slice and strawberries. Top with second piece of cake and layer with banana slices, remaining strawberries and basil. Spread whipped cream on the last square of cake and place on top of basil. Cover and chill. Cut Dessert Club Sandwich from corner to corner, twice, to make 4 portions. Pierce each portion with a fancy toothpick and serve with 4 Pineapple Fries and Strawberry Ketchup. Serve immediately.

● ○ ● ○

SERVES 4

Recipe by Brandon Boone
Photography: Brian Gould

Cranberry Apricot Glace Pie

9" (23 cm) baked pie crust
10–12 sugared, baked, pastry shapes for garnish (optional)
3, 14 oz (398 mL) cans apricot halves, in light syrup, drained – reserve 1 1/2 cups
    (375 mL) syrup
2 tbsp (30 mL) cornstarch
3 tbsp (45 mL) sugar
2 tsp (10 mL) grated orange zest
1 tsp (5 mL) almond extract
1 tbsp (15 mL) butter
1/2 cup (125 mL) dried cranberries
whipped cream (optional)
mint sprigs for garnish

● ● ● ●

Prepare pie crust and pastry garnish.

Drain apricots and reserve syrup. In a medium saucepan, whisk together cornstarch and sugar. Whisk in reserved syrup until no lumps remain. Place pan over medium heat; stir until sauce is thickened and bubbly. Continue to cook and stir for 2 more minutes. Remove from heat. Stir in orange zest, almond extract and butter. Cool. Gently stir in apricots and cranberries. Pour into prepared pie crust. Chill. Serve garnished with baked pastry shapes, whipped cream and mint sprigs.

● ● ● ●

Recipe by Judy Fowler
Photography: Brian Gould

(M)alibu-Infused Wild Cherry & Roasted Hazelnut Pie

Pastry: (Makes enough for 4, 9–10" (23–25 cm)
           pies OR 2 double-crusted pies)
5 1/4 cups (1.31 L) pastry OR all-purpose flour
1 tbsp (15 mL) salt
3/4 cup (175 mL) cold unsalted butter, finely
  cubed
1 3/4 (425 mL) cups vegetable shortening, chilled
1 cup (250 mL) ice water

Malibu-Infused Wild Cherry Filling:
3 lbs (1.5 kg) pitted fresh, wild cherries
1/2 cup (125 mL) Malibu liqueur
1/2 cup (125 mL) flour
3/4 cup (175 mL) sugar
1 tsp (5 mL) salt

Roasted Hazelnut Crumb Topping:
15 plain oatmeal cookies (store bought),
  coarsely crumbled
3 tbsp (45 mL) unsalted butter, melted
3/4 cup (175 mL) sliced hazelnuts

• ◦ • ◦

Pastry: Combine flour and salt in a bowl large enough for you to dig both hands in for mixing. Add butter and, rubbing your hands together, blend dry ingredients and butter until they resemble coarse crumbs. Break up shortening and add it in bits to the mixing bowl. Work shortening into dough so it is in small clumps. Stir in water with a wooden spoon. Turn dough out onto a work surface and gently knead a few times just to pull it together – this is crucial – you don't want to overwork the dough; you want those clumps of shortening intact to create flakes in the crust. Wrap dough in plastic wrap in a log shape and refrigerate for at least 2 hours. Roll out dough on a flour-dusted smooth, cool surface. Make sure to turn dough while rolling it out, to expand it evenly in all directions. Line pie pans with dough; crimp edges with your fingers or a fork and fill with filling.

Filling: Soak cherries in Malibu liqueur for 2 hours. Drain off any remaining liqueur after this time. Combine remaining ingredients in a separate bowl. Toss cherries in the dry mixture.

Topping: Mix together all ingredients.

To Assemble: Pour filling into crust and top with crumb topping. Bake 45 to 60 minutes at 350°F (180°C). Topping should be well browned and firm. Pie crust edge should be golden brown. Cool on wire rack, serve warm or at room temperature.

• ◦ • ◦

Recipe by Nicola Lawson
Photography: Patricia Holdsworth

ick a Pie!

Aphrodite's Pie Pastry:
2 cups (500 mL) all-purpose flour
1/4 tsp (1 mL) salt
1/2 cup (125 mL) non-hydrogenated shortening
1 egg
1/4 cup (60 mL) cold water

Egg Wash:
1 egg
1 tbsp (15 mL) water

Blackberry Apple Pie:
4 cups (1 kg) apples, cored and sliced
2 cups (500 g) blackberries
1/2 cup (125 mL) evaporated
  cane juice OR sugar
2 tbsp (30 mL) arrowroot
1/2 tsp (2 mL) cinnamon

Strawberry Rhubarb Pie:
2 lbs (1 kg) rhubarb, chopped
2 cups (500 g) strawberries, sliced
3/4 cup (125 mL) evaporated cane
  juice OR sugar
3 tbsp (45 mL) arrowroot

● ● ● ●

Pastry: Combine flour, salt and shortening until mixed and crumbly. Add egg and water and stir until combined. Divide dough in half. Roll each piece of dough into an 11" (28 cm) round. Gently place 1 round into a 9" (23 cm) pie plate. Set other round aside until filling is added and then roll out to 11" (23 cm) round.

Egg Wash: Whisk egg and water in a small bowl. Brush over inside of pastry shell.

Filling: Choose your filling. Combine all ingredients in a bowl.

Preheat oven to 350°F (180°C). Place filling in unbaked pie shell. Top with second round of dough and pinch edges, forming a seal. Trim off excess dough. Bake for 30 minutes, or until a probe inserted into the middle of the pie shows clear, not cloudy, juices.

● ● ● ●

Recipe by chef Farhad Mossavad
Photography: Hamid Attie Photography

(S) askatoon Pie

Forget fruit from California, homegrown raspberry-rhubarb and wild blueberry pies are top of the charts at Bread & Circuses.

3 1/2 cups (825 mL) saskatoons
3/4 cup (175 mL) sugar
1/4 cup (60 mL) all-purpose flour
pinch of salt
1 tsp (5 mL) grated lemon zest

• • • •

In a large bowl, combine all ingredients; mix well and pour into a prepared pie shell. For pie crust and baking instructions, please see following page.

• • • •

Recipe by chef Tom Janzen
Photography: Brian Gould

(R) aspberry Rhubarb Pie

1 1/4 cups (300 mL) diced rhubarb
1 1/4 cups (300 mL) raspberries
2/3 cup (150 mL) honey
1 1/2 tbsp (22 mL) cornstarch
1/4 tsp (1 mL) cloves
1/4 tsp (1 mL) salt
1 tbsp (15 mL) grated orange zest

• • • •

In a large bowl, combine all ingredients; mix well and pour into a prepared pie shell. For pie crust and baking instructions, please see following page.

• • • •

Recipe by chef Tom Janzen
Photography: Brian Gould

Bread & Circuses Pie Crust

Aunt Esther's Pie Crust:
3/4 cup (175 mL) all-purpose flour
3/4 cup (175 mL) pastry flour
1/2 tsp (2 mL) salt
1 tbsp (15 mL) brown sugar
1/3 cup (75 mL) butter
1/3 cup (75 mL) vegetable shortening
1/2 egg yolk, beaten
1 tsp (5 mL) vinegar
about 7 tbsp (100 mL) ice-cold water

Tom's Traditional Pie Crust:
1 cup (250 mL) all-purpose flour
1/2 tsp (2 mL) salt
1/4 tsp (1 mL) baking powder
1 tbsp (15 mL) sugar
1/4 cup (60 mL) lard
1/2 cup (125 mL) butter
About 1/2 cup (125 mL) ice cold water

● ● ● ●

For Both Crusts: Preheat oven to 450°F (230°C). Stir dry ingredients together. Cut in shortenings with a pastry blender until mixture is crumbly. Add water a little at a time, using just enough to bind the mixture so dough can be lightly patted to form a ball (handle as little as possible). Roll dough from the centre outward on a lightly floured surface to form a circle 1/8" (3 mm) thick and 1" (2.5 cm) larger than the pie plate. Lift gently into pie plate. Add a generous amount of fruit filling. Fit top crust over filling and lightly press top edge over bottom crust. Trim edges and flute. Cut slits in top for steam to escape. Bake 10 minutes. Reduce heat to 350°F (180°C) and bake 20 to 30 minutes more, until golden and fruit is bubbling.

● ● ● ●

Recipe by chef Tom Janzen

Backyard Rhubarb Cream Pie

This pie is a bubbler, so have a cookie sheet under the pie plate.

pie pastry for a single-crust pie
1 cup (250 mL) sugar
1/3 cup (75 mL) flour
pinch of salt
3/4 cup (175 mL) evaporated milk
8 cups (2 L) chopped rhubarb
4 cups (1 L) oatmeal topping, see page 208 or 209

● ● ● ●

Preheat oven to 425°F (220°C). Roll pastry dough to fit into a 9" (23 cm) wide deep-dish pie plate. Crimp the sides a bit higher than the top edge of the dish. In a bowl, mix together sugar, flour, salt and milk until smooth. Tip rhubarb into pie plate. Dish should be full. Pour cream filling over the fruit. Sprinkle oat topping to cover generously. This should all come just to the top of the crimped pastry. Bake on the bottom rack of oven. The pastry has to cook fast, before it gets soggy. After 20 minutes, check progress. It should be browning. Bake for another 10 to 15 minutes. Reduce heat to 375°F (190°C); bake about 40 minutes, until fruit is tender. If oat topping starts to get too brown, gently cover with foil. The rhubarb must be thoroughly cooked. Cool before slicing. This is best eaten at room temperature, not hot, as the filling needs to set before cutting. It goes beautifully with vanilla ice cream.

● ● ● ●

Recipe by chef Carol Corneau
Photography: John Ulan/Epic Photography

(P)lum Nectarine Galette

Pastry:
2 cups (500 mL) flour
1 tbsp (15 mL) sugar
1/2 tsp (2 mL) salt
grated zest of 1/2 lemon
1/3 cup (75 mL) EACH, cold butter and cold lard
1 egg yolk
1 tsp (5 mL) lemon juice

Filling:
1/2 cup (125 mL) sugar
1/3 cup (75 mL) toasted almonds, sliced, chopped until mealy
1/4 cup (60 mL) flour
pinch salt
14–18 plums
4 nectarines
1 tbsp (15 mL) butter

Plum Nectarine Galette

(continued)

● ◦ ● ◦

Pastry: Preheat oven to 425°F (220°C). Mix together flour, sugar, salt and lemon zest. Using pastry cutter, cut in fats to a fine crumb texture. Beat egg yolk with lemon juice; add enough cold water to make 1/2 cup (125 mL). Pour liquid into dry ingredients all at once and mix gently until dough holds together. Dough should be quite soft but not sticky. Shape into a disk and refrigerate at least 30 minutes.

Filling: Cut plums and nectarines into quarters. Place in large bowl. (If using Italian prune plums use 20; with Santa Rosa or red plums, you may need only 10 to 12 if very large.) Mix together sugar, almonds, flour and salt; stir into the fruit. Don't leave this too long, the sugar will cause fruit to weep and finished galette may end up with soggy pastry.

Grease a 10 to 12" (25 to 30 cm) cast-iron skillet and dust with flour. Use any skillet with high sides, but cast iron really crisps the pastry.

Roll chilled pastry to about a 14" (35 cm) raggedy circle. Pastry should be thicker than regular pies. To make it easier to move, fold pastry in half, lift it from underneath, supporting with your forearm, and place into pan. You want to have a few inches of raggedy pastry to fold over fruit.

Tip fruit into shell and dot with bits of butter. Gently start folding pastry over fruit towards the centre, which should be open. It will look something like a curling rock with pleats/folds of pastry. Brush pastry with a bit of milk and sprinkle with coarse sugar before baking to make it sparkle.

Place galette on bottom rack for 15 minutes; reduce heat to 375°F (190°C) for 35 to 45 minutes. Times are variable depending on pan size; fruit should bubble vigorously and pastry should achieve a deep golden colour. Never underbake fruit pies. When cooked, cool in pan about an hour or until fruit starts to set. Loosen edges with a spatula and firmly give pan a good sharp shake; galette should shift a bit so you can tip it out. Have a large platter ready; grab the pan handle and tip pan toward platter, edge to edge. Shake galette onto platter. Serve at room temperature with whipped cream or ice cream.

● ◦ ● ◦

Recipe by chef Carol Corneau
Photography: John Ulan/Epic Photography

Saskatoon Berry & Fresh Peach Galette

A galette is a flat, open-faced, free-form pie. The crust is rolled into a circle, the filling is piled in the centre and the edges of the crust are turned in and ruffled.

Pastry:
3 tbsp (45 mL) sour cream
1/3 cup (75 mL) ice water
1 cup (250 mL) all-purpose flour
1/4 cup (60 mL) yellow cornmeal
1 tsp (5 mL) sugar
1/2 tsp (2 mL) salt
7 tbsp (105 mL) cold unsalted butter, cut into
     6–8 pieces

Filling:
2 cups (500 mL) fresh saskatoon berries
1 cup (250 mL) fresh peaches, peeled and diced
1/4 cup (60 mL) sugar
2 tbsp (30 mL) honey
2 tbsp (30 mL) cold unsalted butter

● ● ● ●

Pastry: Stir sour cream and water together in a small bowl; set aside. Put flour, cornmeal, sugar and salt in large bowl and stir to mix. Drop butter pieces into bowl, tossing once or twice just to coat with flour. With a pastry blender, work butter into flour, aiming for butter pieces ranging from bread crumbs to small peas. The smaller pieces will make the dough tender, the larger ones will make it flaky.

Sprinkle cold sour cream mixture over dough, about 1 tbsp (15 mL) at a time. Mix with a fork to incorporate liquid. After all sour cream mixture is added, dough should hold together when pressed. If not, add 1 tbsp (15 mL) more water, working in gently. With your hands, gather dough together. Divide dough in half; press each piece into a disk, wrap in plastic wrap and refrigerate for at least 2 hours.

Position a rack in the lower third of oven; preheat oven to 400°F (200°C). Line a baking sheet with parchment paper. On a lightly floured work surface, roll each dough disk into an 11" (28 cm) round. Transfer dough to a baking sheet by rolling dough around a rolling pin. Spread fruit over dough, keeping fruit about 2" (5 cm) away from the edge. Sprinkle sugar, honey and butter cubes over fruit. Lift uncovered dough edges up and over filling, allowing dough to fold naturally and create ruffles. The middle section of fruit will show through the dough "window." Brush dough edges with water and sprinkle with coarse sugar (regular sugar will do).

Bake galette for 35 to 40 minutes, or until pastry is golden and crisp. Serve warm or at room temperature, cutting the galette with a pizza wheel or sharp knife. The galette is best eaten on the day it is made.

● ● ● ●

MAKES 2 GALETTES

Recipe by Nicola Lawson
Photography: Brian Gould

INDEX

LUNCH

Pizzas

Sandwiches

MAIN COURSES

Beef

Fish & Seafood

Lamb

Pasta

Share *FLAVOURS: THE COOKBOOK* with Friends

Order at $24.95 per book plus $5.00 (total order) for postage and handling.

Flavours: The Cookbook _____ x $24.95 = $ _____

Postage and handling _____ = $ _____5.00_____

Subtotal _____ = $ _____

In Canada add 6% GST _____(Subtotal x .06) = $ _____

Total enclosed _____ = $ _____

U.S. and international orders payable in U.S. funds./Price is subject to change

NAME _____

STREET _____

CITY_____ PROV./STATE _____

POSTAL CODE/ZIP _____ TELEPHONE _____

E-MAIL_____

❑ CHEQUE   OR   Charge to   ❑ VISA   ❑ MASTERCARD

Account Number: _____

Expiry Date: (month) _____   (year) _____

Make completed order and payment to:
Centax Books & Distribution, 1150 Eighth Avenue, Regina, SK, Canada S4R 1C9
Or order by Toll-Free Phone: 1-800-667-5595 or by Toll-Free Fax: 1-800-823-6829
E-mail: centax@printwest.com   website: centaxbooks.com

**See our website for our complete range of
cookbooks, gardening books, history books, etc.
www.centaxbooks.com**

For fund-raising or volume purchases, contact Centax Books & Distribution
for volume rates. Please allow 2-3 weeks for delivery.